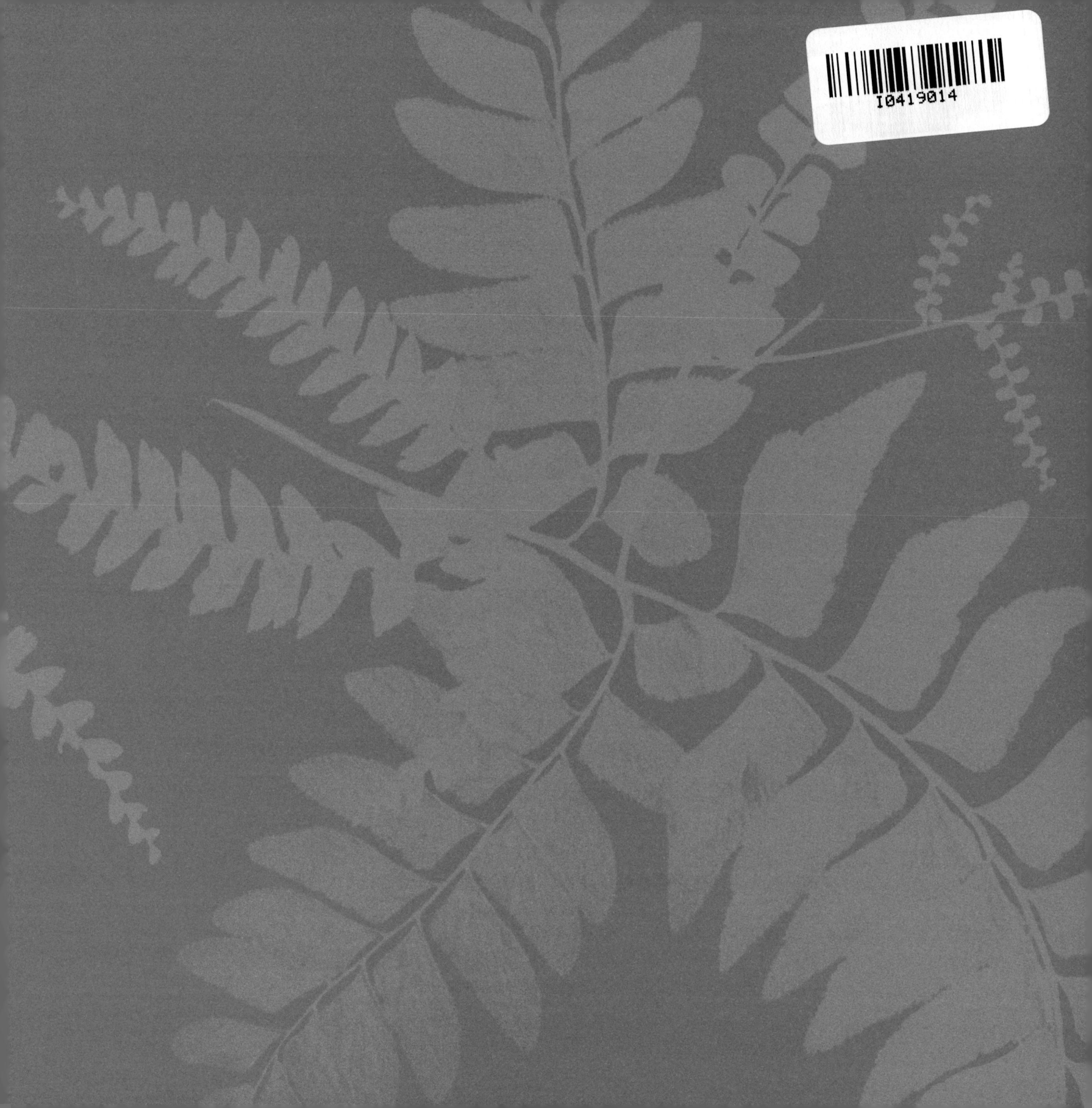

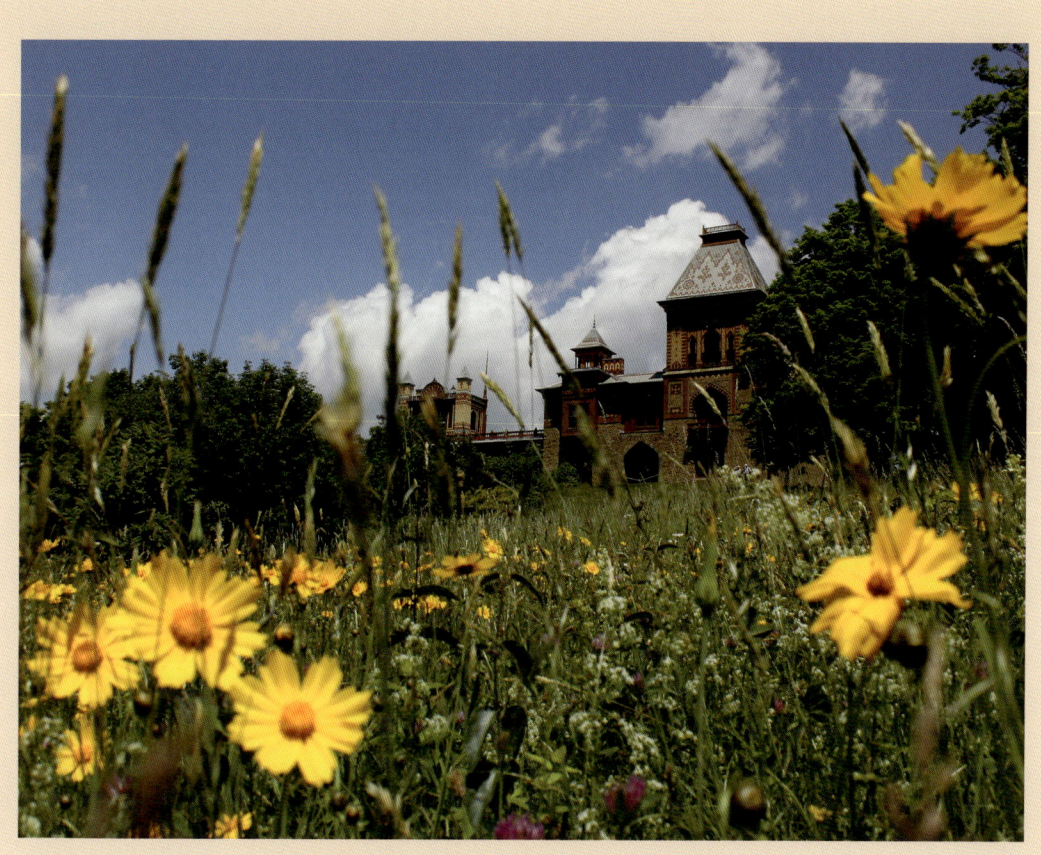

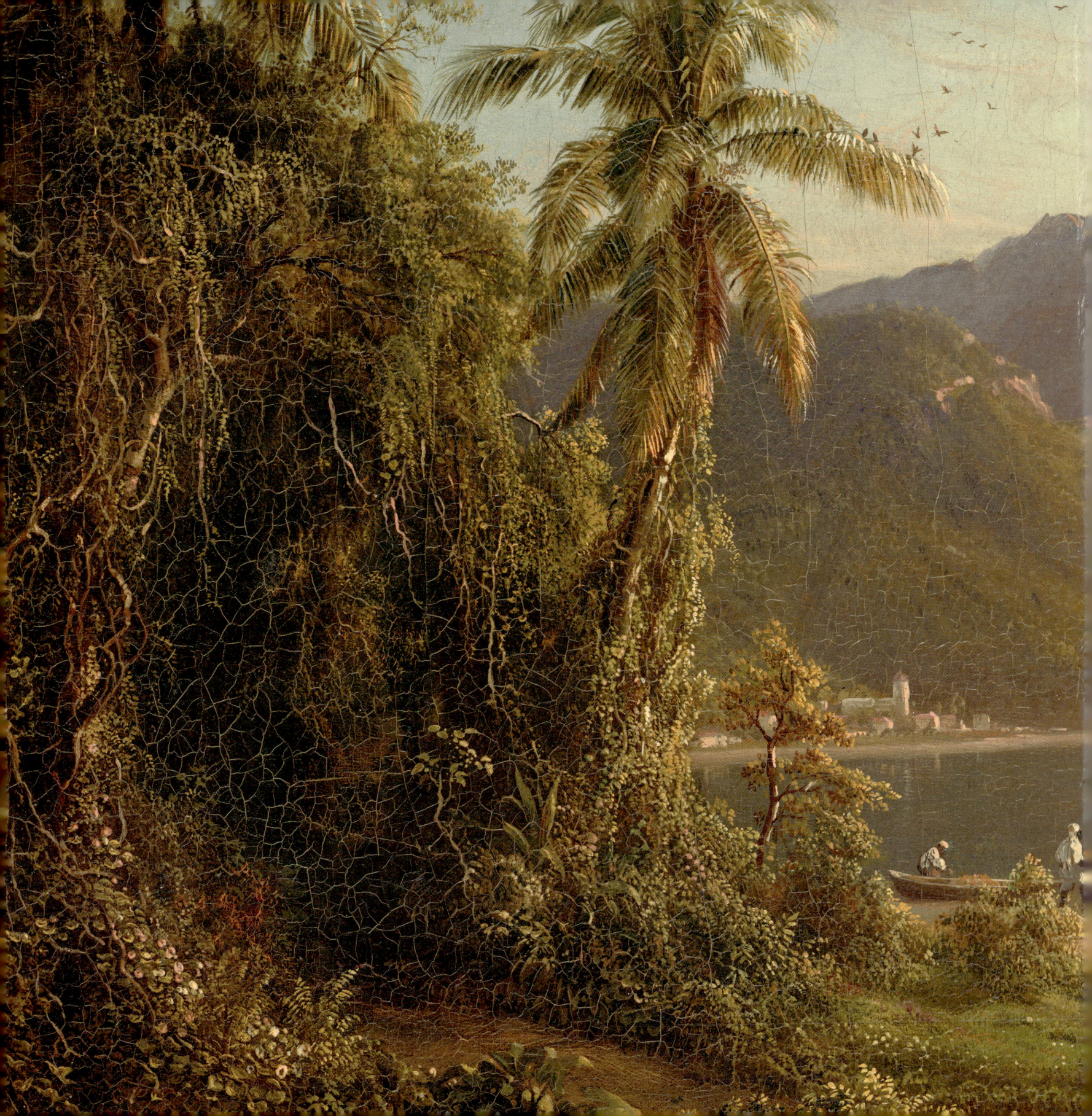

Fern Hunting among These Picturesque Mountains

Frederic Edwin Church in Jamaica

ESSAYS BY ELIZABETH MANKIN KORNHAUSER
AND KATHERINE E. MANTHORNE

FOREWORD BY ANTHONY JOHNSON

FERN HUNTING AMONG THESE PICTURESQUE MOUNTAINS
IS THE 2010 EXHIBITION IN THE
EVELYN AND MAURICE SHARP GALLERY AT OLANA

THE OLANA PARTNERSHIP
HUDSON, NEW YORK

NEW YORK STATE OFFICE OF PARKS, RECREATION
AND HISTORIC PRESERVATION
ALBANY, NEW YORK

CORNELL UNIVERSITY PRESS
ITHACA AND LONDON

This exhibition, *Fern Hunting among These Picturesque Mountains: Frederic Edwin Church in Jamaica*, was organized by The Olana Partnership and the New York State Office of Parks, Recreation and Historic Preservation, using objects from the collection of Olana State Historic Site, Hudson, New York.

Olana State Historic Site is one of 35 historic properties administered and operated by the New York State Office of Parks, Recreation and Historic Preservation: David A. Paterson, Governor.

Unless otherwise credited, all photographs and other visual images are courtesy of Olana State Historic Site, New York State Office of Parks, Recreation and Historic Preservation.

Library of Congress Cataloging-in-Publication Data
Church, Frederic Edwin, 1826–1900.
    Fern hunting among these picturesque mountains :
Frederic Edwin Church in Jamaica / essays by Elizabeth Mankin Kornhauser and Katherine E. Manthorne ; foreword by Anthony Johnson.
      p. cm.
    "Fern hunting among these picturesque mountains is the 2010 exhibition in the Evelyn and Maurice Sharp Gallery at Olana."
    Includes bibliographical references.
    ISBN 978-0-8014-4920-8 (cloth : alk. paper)
    1. Church, Frederic Edwin, 1826–1900—Exhibitions.
2. Jamaica—In art—Exhibitions. 3. Landscape painting, American—19th century—Exhibitions. I. Kornhauser, Elizabeth Mankin, 1950– II. Manthorne, Katherine. III. Evelyn and Maurice Sharp Gallery. IV. Olana Partnership. V. New York (State). Office of Parks, Recreation, and Historic Preservation. VI. Title.
  ND237.C52A4 2010
  759.13—dc22   2010005694

First published 2010 by The Olana Partnership and Cornell University Press.

Endsheets: Isabel Carnes Church, *Pressed Ferns in an Herbarium* (detail), OL.2001.76

Page 1: Carri Manchester, *Olana with Coreopsis in Bloom*, 2009 (detail, see fig. 3)

Pages 2–3: Frederic Edwin Church, *Jamaica*, 1871 (detail, see fig. 29)

Pages 4–5: Frederic Edwin Church, *Blue Mountains, Jamaica*, c. July–August 1865 (detail, see fig. 23)

Page 6: Unknown photographer, *Louis Church Walking by the Fern Bed, North of the Main House at Olana*, c. 1885–1914 (detail, see fig. 16)

Page 10: Frederic Edwin Church, *Fern Walk, Jamaica*, July 1865 (detail, see fig. 14)

Page 68: Frederic Edwin Church, *Sunset, Jamaica*, July 1865 (see fig. 28)

Page 70: Nicholas Whitman, *East Facade, Olana*, photograph, 2001, nwphoto.com

Page 72: Nicholas Whitman, *View from the Piazza at Olana*, 2001 (see fig. 55), nwphoto.com

Edited by Lory Frankel
Proofread by Alarik Skarstrom and Laura Iwasaki
Designed by John Hubbard
Typeset by Marie Weiler
Color management by iocolor, Seattle
Produced by Marquand Books, Inc., Seattle
  www.marquand.com
Printed and bound in China by C&C Offset Printing Co., Ltd.

Contents

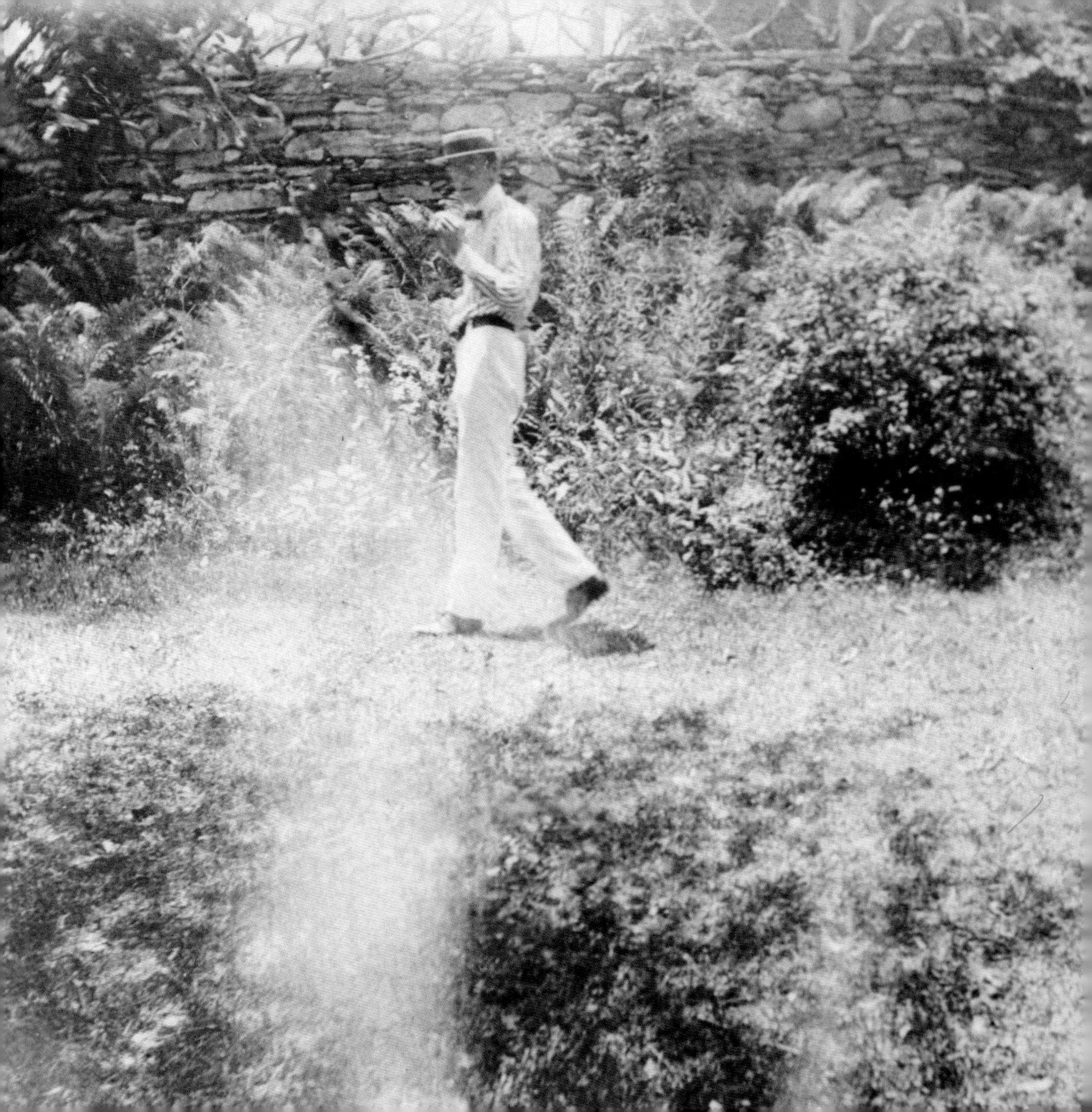

Preface and Acknowledgments

In 1865, Frederic Edwin Church, an avid traveler with a special passion for the tropics, journeyed to Jamaica. This was unlike his previous excursions, as he and his wife, Isabel, were escaping from intense personal grief: the loss of two of their children. Throwing himself into exploring the island and recording its details and scenes, the renowned artist produced a variety of works ranging from delicate pen sketches of palm trees to oil sketches of the atmospheric Blue Mountains and brilliant sunsets. Jamaica provided distraction for both Frederic, who "accomplished a great amount of work," and Isabel, who was "fascinated with the occupation of fern collecting," and they encouraged friends to join them in "fern hunting among these picturesque Mountains," as Church reported to Theodore Cole in a letter of July 28, 1865 (OL.1981.863).

The importance of the trip is reflected in the number of studies Church chose to mount, frame, and display at Olana. One of his major Jamaican canvases, *The After Glow*, 1867, which was originally sold to his parents, later became a major attraction for visitors to his home. The Evelyn and Maurice Sharp Gallery at Olana is the perfect place to examine these beautiful works closely.

This year, in conjunction with the exhibition and in tribute to Frederic and Isabel's visit to Jamaica, The Olana Partnership is restoring the fern bed at Olana. This area of Church's landscape was a sanctuary for native ferns on the north side of the house. Undoubtedly, after viewing Isabel's pressed ferns and Frederic's sketches, visitors to the Churches' home wandered along the "fern walk."

Olana is Church's masterpiece. It is the perfect blend of exotic architecture, the artful display of collections, and a romantic landscape—a microcosm of all of the artist's interests. We are pleased to be able to present an exhibition of Church's Jamaican works, organized and curated by The Olana Partnership Curator Evelyn D. Trebilcock and Associate Curator Valerie A. Balint and researched by Librarian/Archivist Ida Brier, with research assistance by Curatorial Interns Alexandra Anderson and Danielle Swanson, along with a revived part of the landscape that is directly linked to the exhibition.

Fern Hunting among These Picturesque Mountains: Frederic Edwin Church in Jamaica and the accompanying exhibition represent a tremendous joint effort on the part of the New York State Office of Parks, Recreation and Historic Preservation and its non-profit partner, The Olana Partnership. Together these two institutions are working to preserve and restore Olana—the crown jewel of the Hudson River Valley.

We thank the following for their help with this exhibition: New York State Governor David A. Paterson; New York State Office of Parks, Recreation and Historic Preservation Commissioner Carol Ash; Deputy Commissioner for Historic Preservation J. Winthrop Aldrich; Regional Director, Taconic Region, Jayne McLaughlin; and at Olana State Historic Site, Site Manager Linda E. McLean and Interpretive Programs Assistant Carri Manchester. We are also grateful to The Olana Partnership staff members: President Sara Griffen; Curator Evelyn D. Trebilcock; Associate Curator Valerie A. Balint; Librarian/Archivist Ida Brier; Curatorial Interns Alexandra Anderson and Danielle Swanson; Vice President for Development Robert Burns; Director of Administration and Public Affairs Nelson Sterner; and Executive Assistant Mary Curran.

For providing their thoughts on Church and his fellow painters in Jamaica and the tropics, we thank Elizabeth Mankin Kornhauser and Katherine E. Manthorne. We appreciate Anthony Johnson's lovely foreword, where he shares his perspective on Church, Jamaica, and the wonderful ferns that inhabit his island. For preparing the paintings, photographs, and printed material for display and photographic materials for this publication, we are grateful to the New York State Office of Parks, Recreation and Historic Preservation Peebles Island Resource Center staff: Acting Director for the Bureau of Historic Sites John Lovell; Director of the Division for Historic Preservation Ruth Pierpont; Collections Manager Anne Ricard Cassidy and her staff Erin Czernecki, Ronna Dixson, and Mary Zaremski; Former Curator Robin Campbell, Curator Susan Walker, and Assistant Curator Amanda Massie; Paper Conservator Michele Phillips; Frames Conservator Eric Price; Paintings Conservator Joyce Zucker; and Photographer Richard Clauss.

The catalogue, which will serve to enlighten readers about the collections at Olana, the adventures of Frederic and Isabel Church, and the lure of Jamaica long after the exhibition closes, would not have been possible without early support from Henry and Sharon Martin or the guidance of Ed Marquand and his staff at Marquand Books. For their continued support of Olana publications, we are grateful to Cornell University Press, especially John Ackerman and his staff. We acknowledge Lory Frankel for her thoughtful editing of the essays and Alarik Skarstrom and Laura Iwasaki for their careful attention to the proofs. For supporting images we thank John Benicewicz at Art Resource, New York; Jonathan Boos; Kayla Carlsen at Christie's; Elizabeth Saluk at The Cleveland Museum of Art; Jacquelann Killian and Chuck Kim at the Cooper-Hewitt, National Design Museum, New York, Smithsonian Institution; Fiona Bradley at the Royal Botanic Gardens, Kew; Richard Manoogian; Cheryl Robledo at the Manoogian Collection; Susan Grinols at the Fine Arts Museums of San Francisco; Meghan Mazella and Erin Schleigh at The Museum of Fine Arts, Boston; Franklin Kelly, Deputy Director and Chief Curator, National Gallery of Art, Washington, D.C.; Eleanor Gillers and Jill Slaight at the New-York Historical Society; Private Collection; Chloe Richfield, Director, and Louis M. Salerno, Owner, Questroyal Fine Art, LLC; Mike Ramos; and Erin Monroe and Allen Phillips at the Wadsworth Atheneum Museum of Art. For contemporary images of Olana included here, we thank photographers Kurt Dolnier, Carri Manchester, and Nicholas Whitman.

For their advice, support, and encouragement of the exhibition, the Evelyn and Maurice Sharp Gallery at Olana, and this publication, we want to recognize the Olana Curatorial Committee: Susan Winokur, Chair; Armin B. Allen; Stephen Edidin, Chief Curator, New-York Historical Society; Barry Harwood, Curator of Decorative Arts, Brooklyn Museum of Art; Mary Ellen Hern, Director of Development, New York State Historical Association, Fenimore Art Museum, and The Farmers' Museum; Judith Hernstadt; Frederick D. Hill; Paul Leach; John Lovell, Peebles Island Resource Center; Linda E. McLean, Olana State Historic Site; Carri Manchester, Olana State Historic Site; Amy G. Poster, Curator Emerita of Asian Art, Brooklyn Museum of Art; Richard T. Sharp; Carol Irish Strone, Carol Strone Art Advisory; and Karen Zukowski, Independent Scholar.

Finally, we wish to thank the generous individual and institutional donors who provided the necessary funds that have made this important book and exhibition possible: Mr. and Mrs. Brock Ganeles; David G. Kabiller; Henry and Sharon Martin; the Lois H. and Charles A. Miller Jr. Foundation; Chas. A. Miller III; the New York State Council on the Arts Museum Program; The Reed Foundation; Richard T. Sharp; the Terra Foundation for American Art; the Jack Warner Fund for Creativity and Innovation; Susan Winokur and Paul Leach; and the Olana Exhibition Fund.

The second exhibition in the Evelyn and Maurice Sharp Gallery at Olana, *Fern Hunting among These Picturesque Mountains: Frederic Edwin Church in Jamaica* reflects Olana's continued commitment to increasing Church scholarship and giving the public access to the collection.

Washburn S. Oberwager
Chair, The Olana Partnership

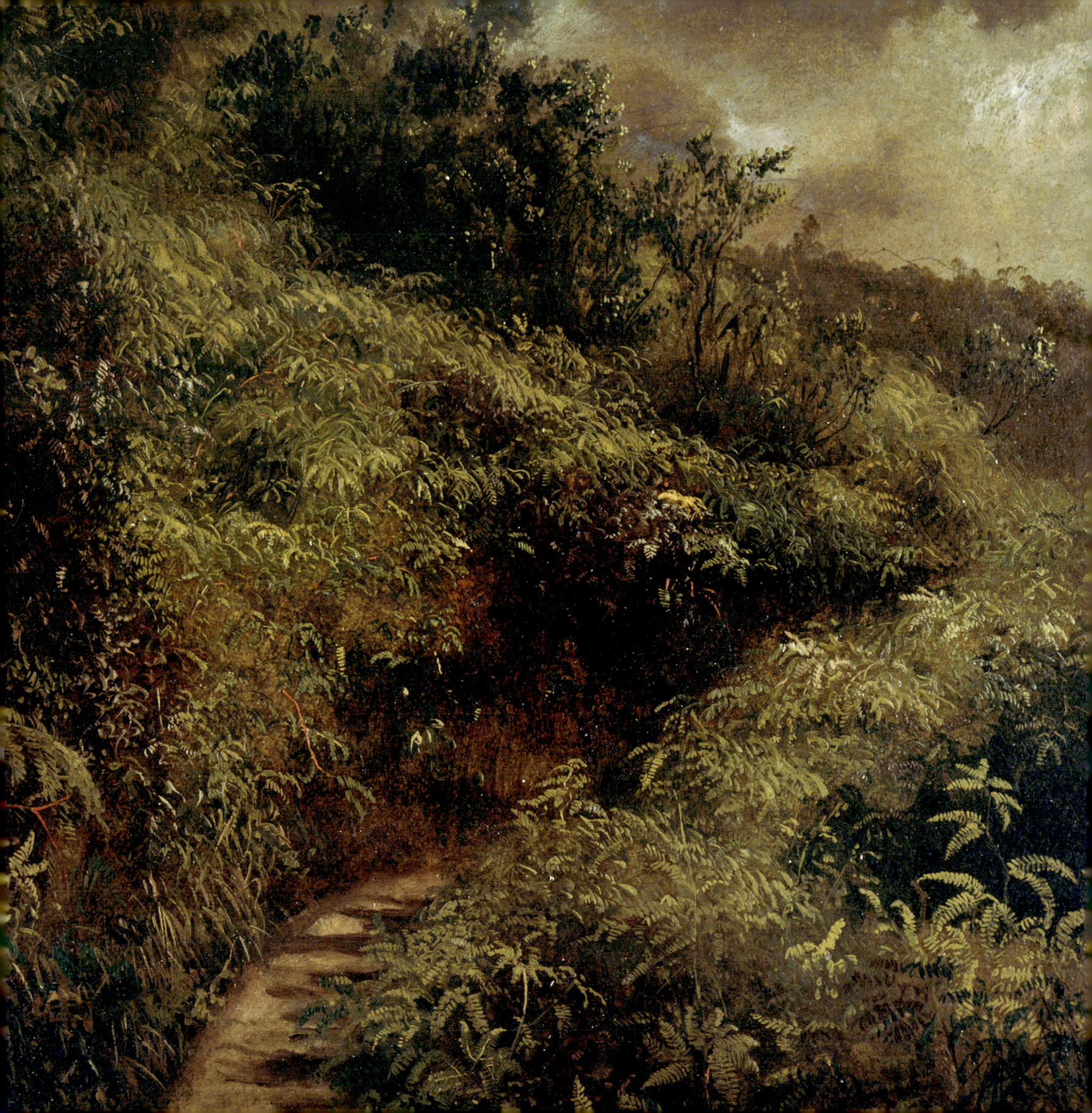

Foreword

Almost a century and a half has passed since the monumental events of 1865 shook the foundations of both the United States and Jamaica, its small island neighbor.

In the United States, that year saw the climax of the great struggle between North and South, freedom and captivity, industrial might versus agrarian traditionalism. In Jamaica, it saw an eruption of newly freed black settlers against injustice and a threat to their livelihoods. In both countries, much blood was spilled in the fight for these basic human rights.

This book deals not with these fundamental issues of 1865, but rather with a long-ago family journey that awakened a particular aesthetic response in a handful of individuals. Olana has decided to present an account of this venture, in which metropolitan aesthetes, inspired by the tropical island, developed new artistic material. This was incorporated into the work of an artistic giant, whose oeuvre is central to one of the Western world's great artistic movements.

Art historians have long since documented the growth of indigenous artistic styles in the Western Hemisphere, weaned from their European sources and solidly based on the life forms and geographic attributes of their native habitats. This book focuses on two artistic pursuits in the island of Jamaica, totally unrelated to the sugar, rum, and codfish trades that had been the basis of commerce for three centuries between New England and the Caribbean.

The first influenced the majestic oil paintings of Frederic Edwin Church (1826–1900), and the second concerned the delicate, and mostly forgotten, intricate craft of dried flower arrangements based on ferns.

The Church saga is well worth telling. The great landscape master had developed his skills in the Hudson Valley, studying with the most famous landscape painter of the time, Thomas Cole (1801–1848). Along with other artists who shared their vision of painting, they formed what is now known as the Hudson River School, the first widely accepted indigenous American school of painting.

Church was born to a well-off family, and fame came early to him. Crowds lined the sidewalks of New York and paid a few cents to gaze in awe at his magnificent canvases. His brush presented the grandeur and potential of the Americas to the young population, bringing him adulation and greater wealth.

But there was a snake in the garden. Church was at the height of his fame when his two young children succumbed to diphtheria in early 1865. Devastated by grief, he and his wife, Isabel, heeded a suggestion that they go on a journey and try to forget. With a few friends, they set off for Jamaica.

The therapy worked. In five hectic summer months, the Churches explored the mountains of Jamaica, absorbing the warm, refreshing breezes, studying the new shades and hues of the blazing sun, the craggy mountains, and hundreds of exotic shrubs and trees. Church relied on his genius for sketching to fill hundreds of pages with pencil and ink drawings of details and scenes that caught his fancy.

After this experience, he produced marvelous paintings that have thrilled millions across the globe. His interest in South America, the Arctic, and the Middle East is well known. We here pay tribute to another influence—the Isle of Springs, Jamaica.

While Frederic was busy mastering the macro-environment, Isabel was just as busy investigating the micro-elements in the form of flowers, shrubs, and whatever flora she thought would produce decorative designs. As she delved into this popular nineteenth-century hobby, like her husband, she found the Jamaican countryside to be a bonanza for useful harvesting.

Isabel's notebooks containing beautiful and intricate floral designs are in the collection of Olana and have been carefully preserved over the last century and a half.

The fern craze brought many other ladies to Jamaica, but few, if any, have left such a large intact collection of works that may still be viewed and admired.

The story ends happily, with Frederic fully restored to creativity and vitality and Isabel producing another son, followed by two more sons and a daughter, all of whom survived to continue the family line.

For those who love Jamaica and the Caribbean, the exhibition presented at Olana, Frederic Church's beautiful, picturesque home on the Hudson, in the Evelyn and Maurice Sharp Gallery, and its accompanying publication furnish material for several observations. They bear witness to the lasting effect that Jamaican scenes had on the post-1865 works of Church, at the same time that they showcase the dramatic effect of Jamaican scenery, which has continued to please millions of Americans who visit the islands to discover new aspects of tropical beauty.

As for the humble, often forgotten ferns, hundreds of varieties live on in Jamaica. The once magnificent Fern Gully (or Fern Walk, as Church described it) still exists, gasping for life under the constant abuse of automotive exhaust fumes. Strange irony that the geological "age of ferns," which produced the seed material for the billions of barrels of fossil fuels that have brought so much convenience and comfort to the modern world, should now be also threatening to destroy the natural environment celebrated by this exhibition. It is hoped that this publication will help encourage the restoration and preservation of some of the beautiful areas of Jamaica, so that they appear once again as they did when Frederic and Isabel Church visited the island.

Enjoy.

Anthony Johnson, FRSA,
Jamaica's Ambassador to the United States

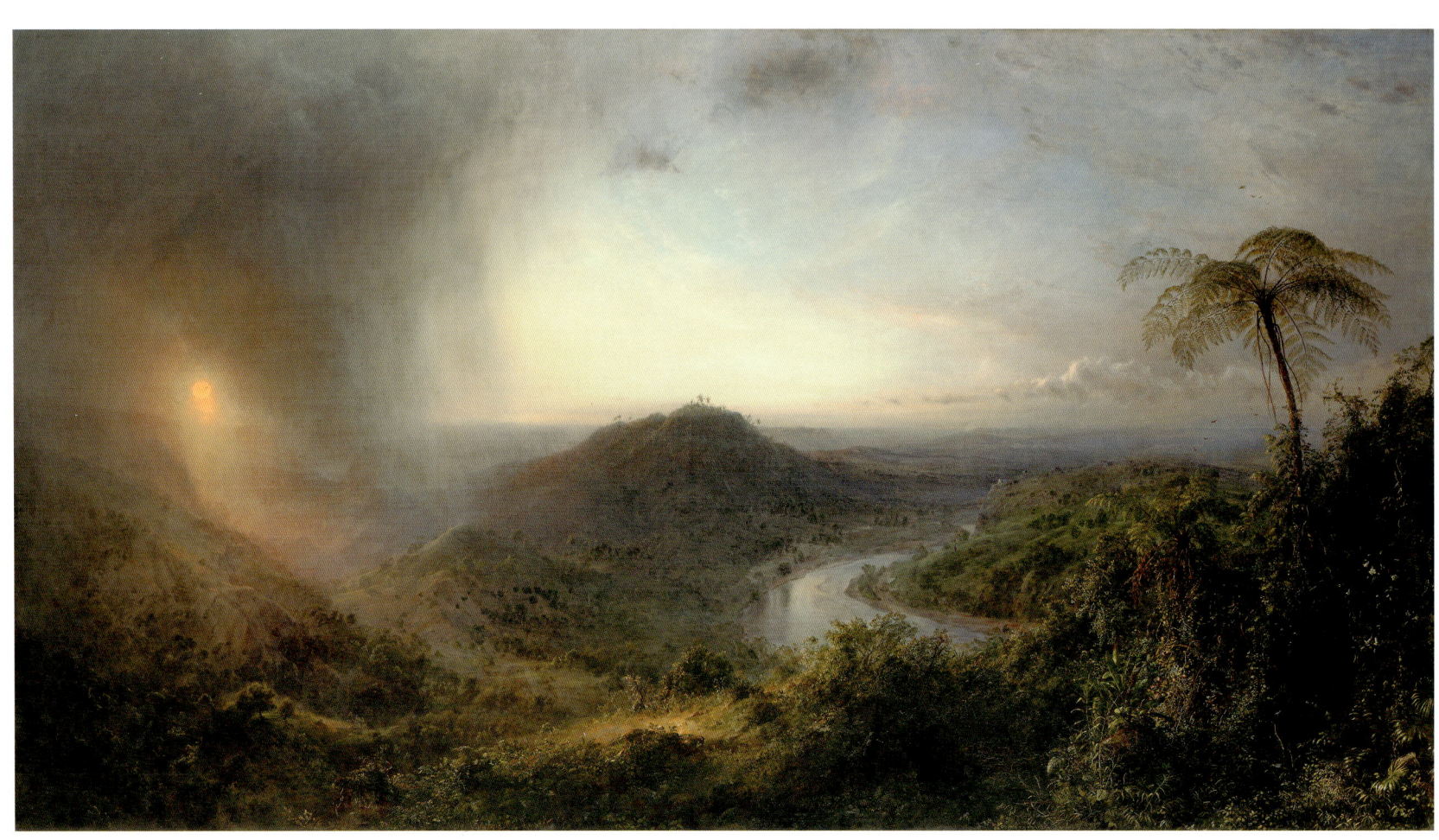

Elizabeth Mankin Kornhauser

Frederic Edwin Church's Landscapes of Jamaica

In April 1865, shaken by a recent personal tragedy, Frederic Edwin Church (1826–1900) left for Jamaica on a sketching trip. The journey, set against the traumatic events of the Civil War as well as racial tensions Church encountered on the island of Jamaica, served as a continuation of his life's work to capture the grandeur of the earth's creation in his landscapes of the New World. The most important of the many landscapes he painted of this tropical island, *The Vale of St. Thomas, Jamaica*, was commissioned by a close friend of the artist and a resident of his native city, Hartford, Connecticut (fig. 1). In addition, Church made hundreds of drawings and oil studies of the island of extraordinary quality (fig. 2). These, and the oil compositions based on his sketches that he painted on his return, also reflect the tensions that provided the backdrop for his journey. Many of these rich and deeply meaningful works from the Jamaican trip remain at the artist's home, Olana (fig. 3).

This was not just another trip in search of fresh inspiration following his series of acclaimed tropical landscapes.[1] Church's departure occurred during the final stages of the Civil War and just days after the assassination of President Abraham Lincoln on April 14. Cognizant of this national tragedy, Church (fig. 4) and his wife, Isabel (1836–1899; fig. 5), also suffered a devastating personal loss. A month earlier, their two children, Herbert, age two, and Emma, age five months, died from diphtheria. The artist memorialized their births and deaths in two small oils, *Sunrise*, 1862, and *Moonrise*, 1865, eventually hanging them in the Sitting Room at Olana, where they remain (fig. 6). The need to escape their familial surroundings in search of spiritual renewal likely instigated the journey. As the arts writer and critic Henry Tuckerman recorded, "domestic affliction rendering a change of scene desirable," the Churches set sail for Jamaica on April 22, in the company of several friends, including the young artist Horace Wolcott Robbins (who had roots in Hartford) and his friend Sarah Hitchcock and the Danish artist Fritz Melbye, for a five-month sojourn.[2]

Fig. 1. Frederic Edwin Church, *The Vale of St. Thomas, Jamaica*, 1867, oil on canvas, 48⁵⁄₁₆ × 84⅝ in., Wadsworth Atheneum Museum of Art, Hartford, Conn., Bequest of Elizabeth Hart Jarvis Colt, 1905.21

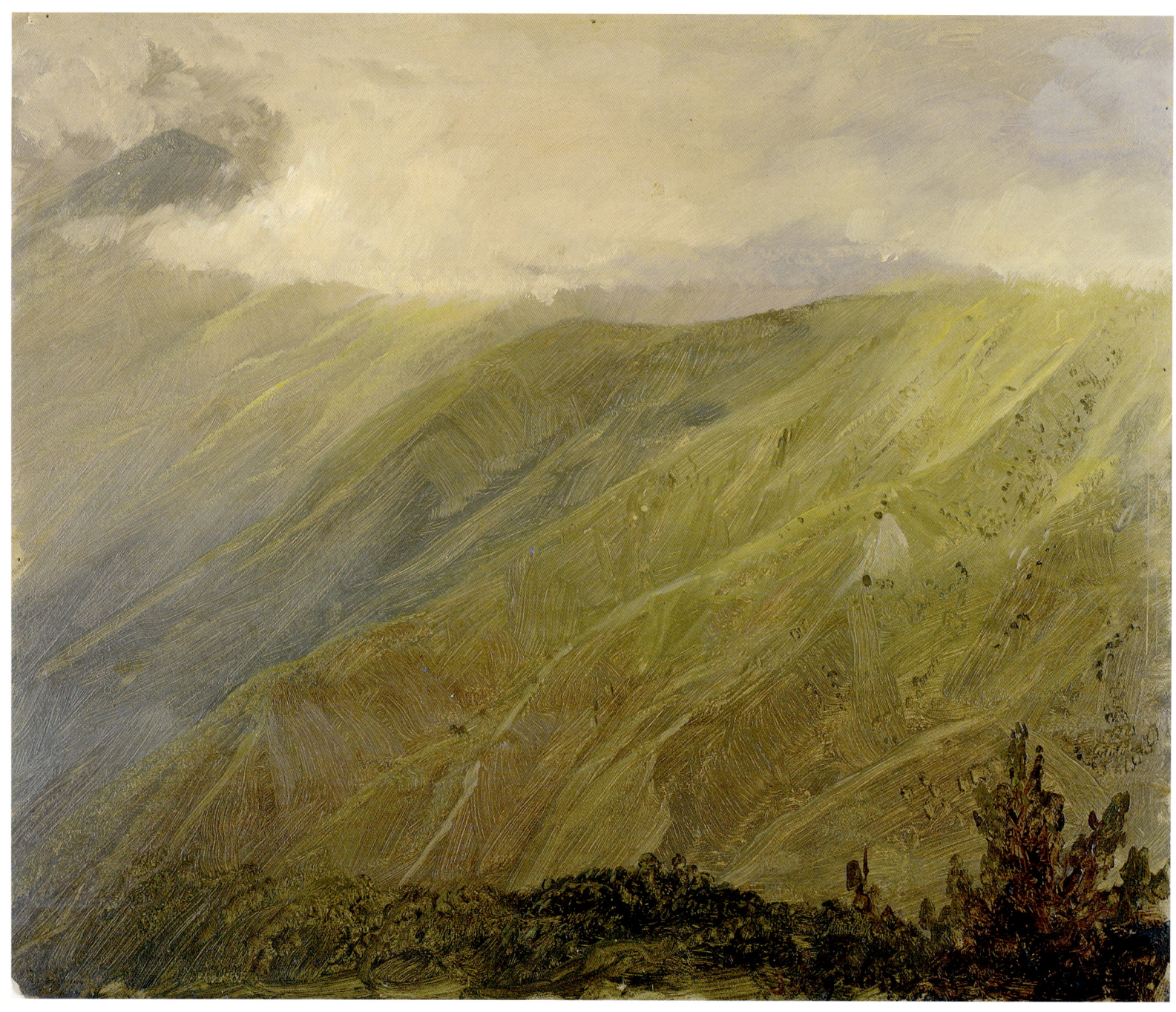

Fig. 2. Frederic Edwin Church, *Ridges in the Blue Mountains, Jamaica*, July 1865, oil on paper, 10⅜ × 12 1/16 in., OL.1976.3

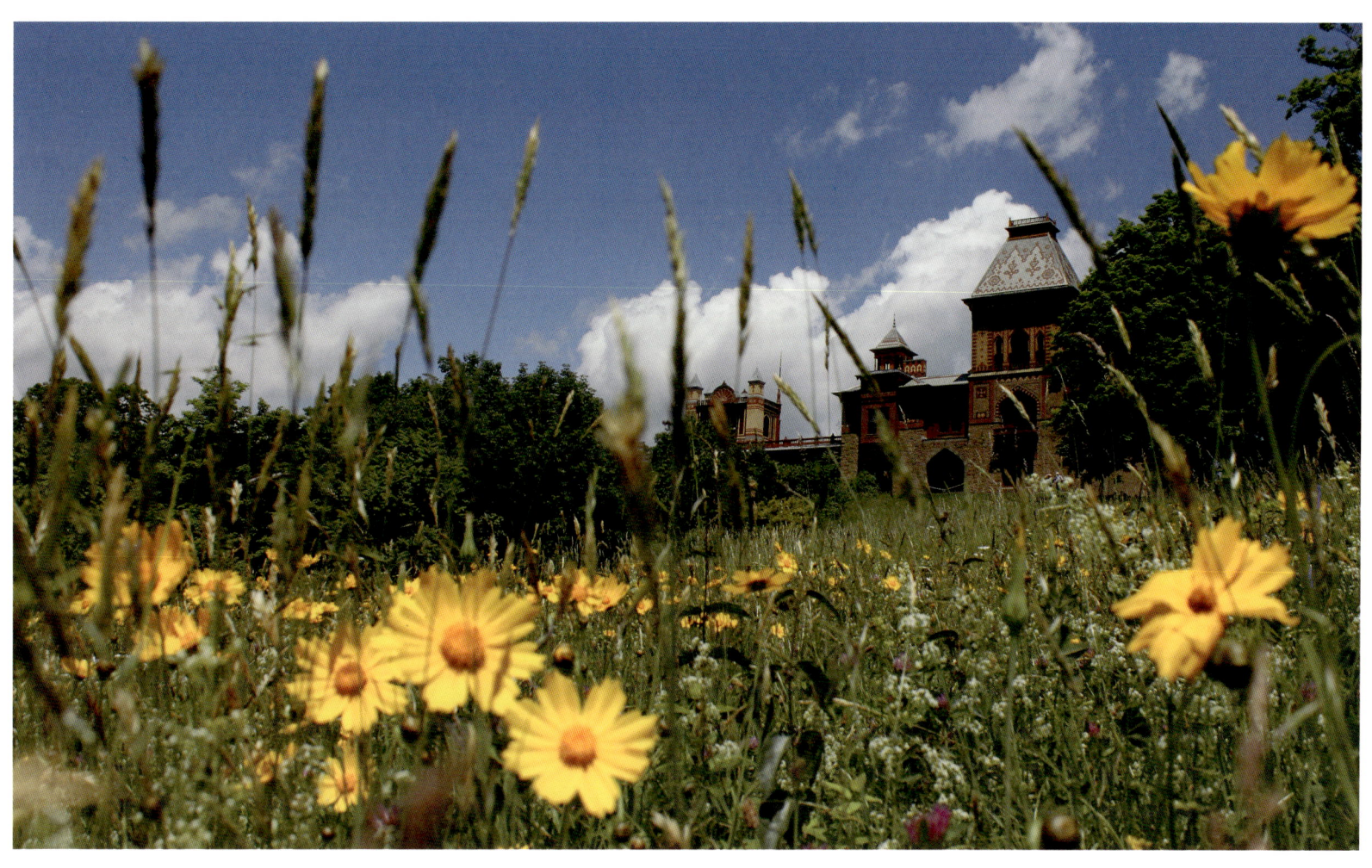

Fig. 3. Carri Manchester, *Olana with Coreopsis in Bloom*, photograph, 2009

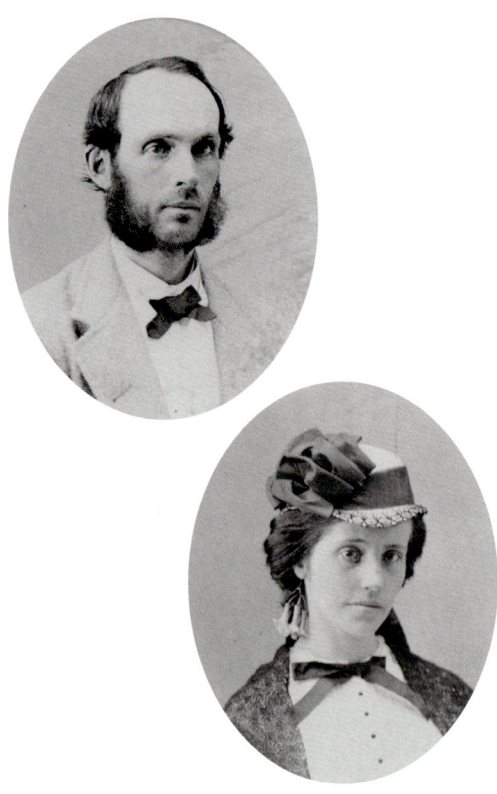

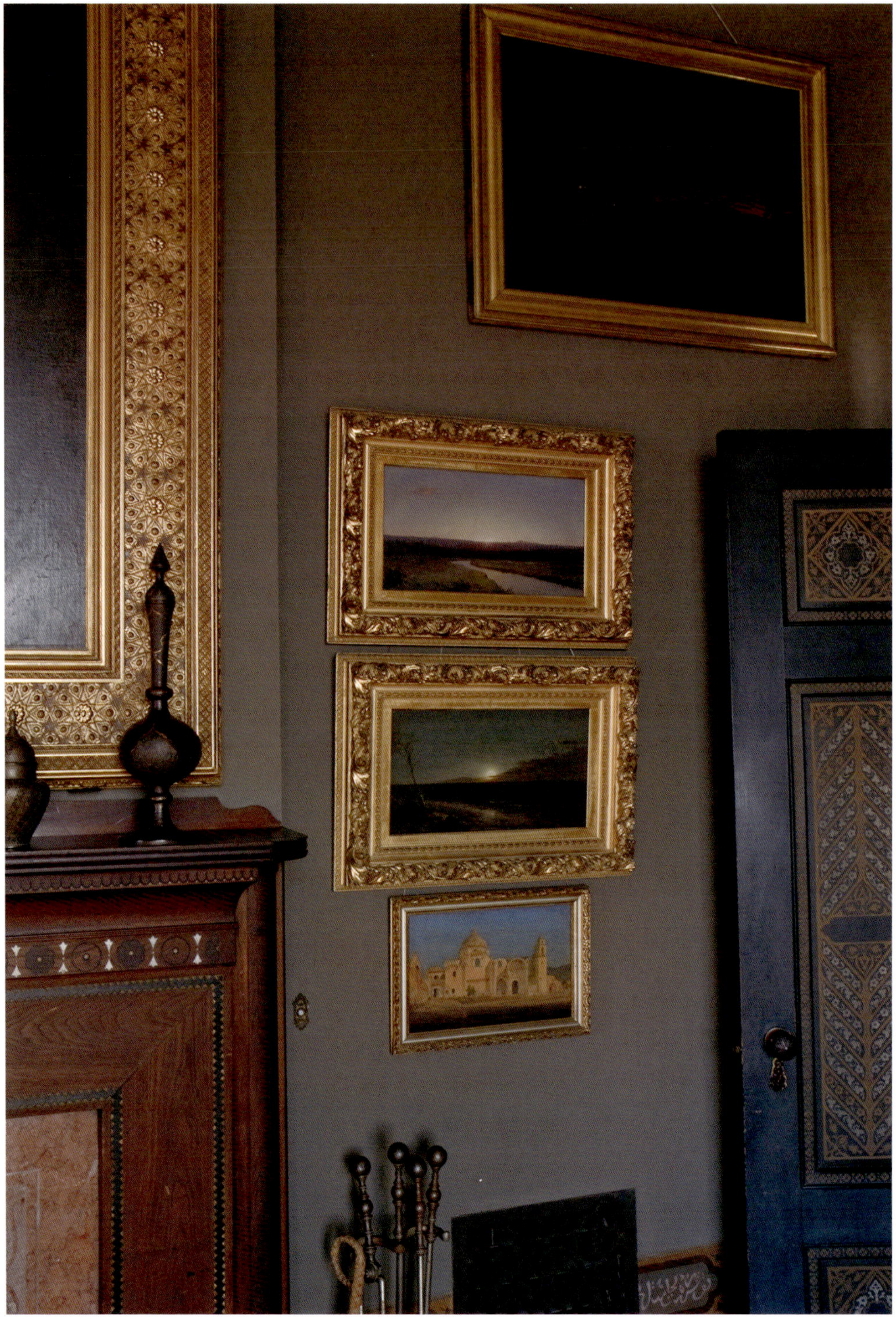

Fig. 4. Freeman Studio, *Frederic Edwin Church*, 1865, tintype (oval format) taken in Kingston, Jamaica, 4⅝ × 2⅜ in., OL.1992.7.1

Fig. 5. Freeman Studio, *Isabel Carnes Church*, 1865, tintype (oval format) taken in Kingston, Jamaica, 4 × 2⅜ in., OL.1992.10.1

Fig. 6. Nicholas Whitman, *"Sunrise" and "Moonrise" on View in the Sitting Room at Olana*, photograph, 2009, nwphoto.com

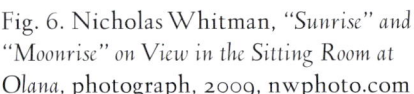

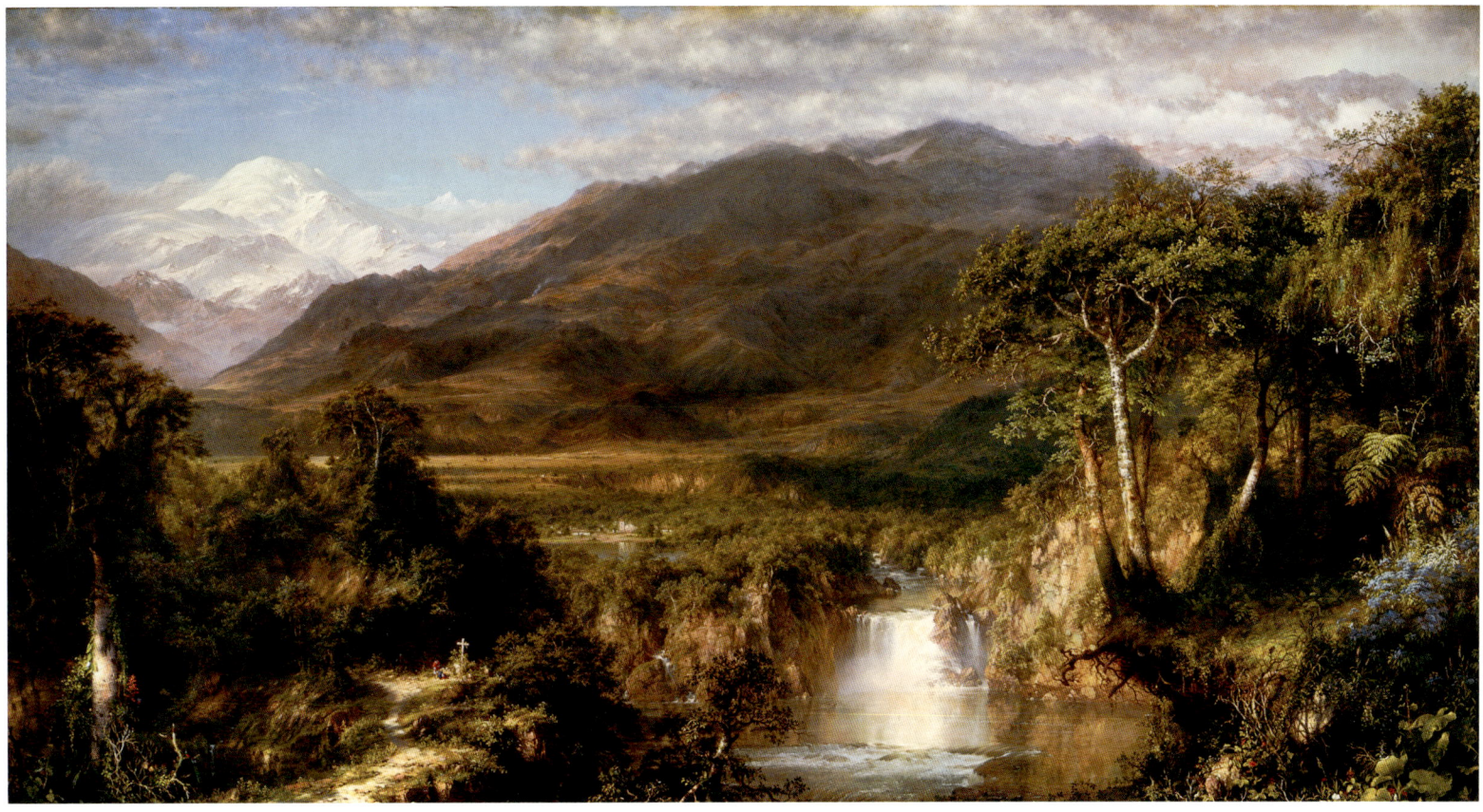

At age thirty-nine, as an internationally acclaimed artist, Church had completed a series of paintings that scholars consider his greatest works, including *Niagara*, 1857 (Corcoran Gallery of Art, Washington, D.C.), *The Heart of the Andes*, 1859 (fig. 7), *Twilight in the Wilderness*, 1860 (fig. 8), *The Icebergs*, 1861 (Dallas Museum of Art), *Cotopaxi*, 1862 (Detroit Institute of Arts), and *Coast Scene, Mount Desert*, 1863 (Wadsworth Atheneum Museum of Art, Hartford, Connecticut). The harrowing years of the Civil War had drawn Church into a number of national roles in support of the Union army and the abolitionist movement. Many of his works from this time have been interpreted by scholars as responding, in part, to the impending Civil War and its eventual eruption.[3] Perhaps the best measure of the artist's involvement in the nation's strife can be seen in his reaction when he learned that on April 12, 1861, the gun batteries of South Carolina had opened fire on Fort Sumter. He was just about to place his masterful *The Icebergs* at the Goupil Gallery, in New York, for public viewing, and on hearing the news, he pointedly changed the title to *The North*. On behalf of the Union cause, Church directed that the monies raised from the exhibition be donated to the Patriotic Fund recently established in support of Union soldiers. He then painted the politically charged work

Fig. 7. Frederic Edwin Church, *The Heart of the Andes*, 1859, oil on canvas, 66⅛ × 119¼ in., The Metropolitan Museum of Art, New York, Bequest of Margaret E. Dows, 1909, 09.95, Image © The Metropolitan Museum of Art/Art Resource, NY

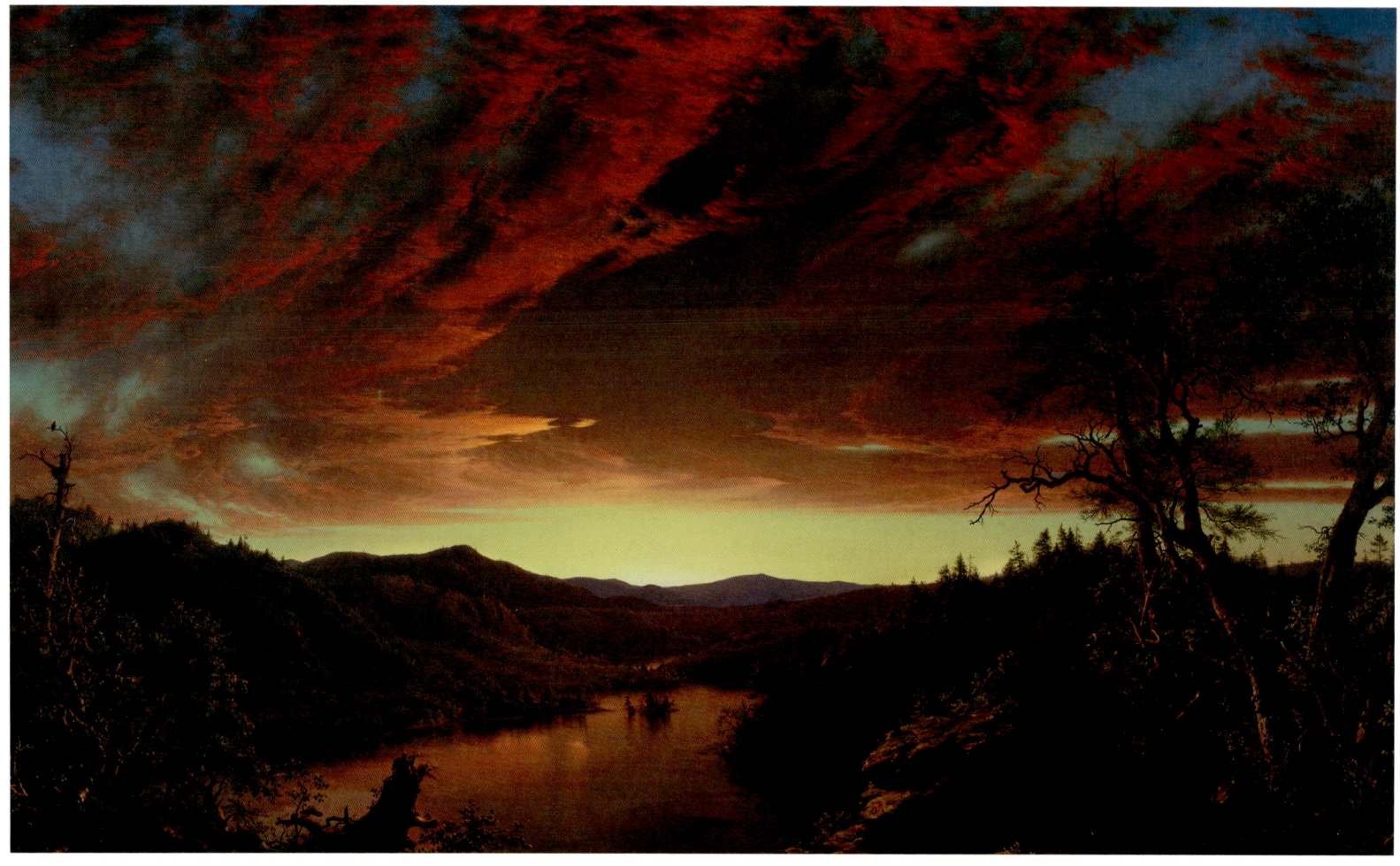

Fig. 8. Frederic Edwin Church, *Twilight in the Wilderness*, 1860, oil on canvas, 40 × 64 in., The Cleveland Museum of Art, Mr. and Mrs. William H. Marlatt Fund, 1965.233, Image © The Cleveland Museum of Art

Our Banner in the Sky, April–May 1861, which depicted the torn United States flag, and placed it alongside *The Icebergs* at the Goupil Gallery by late May, with an accompanying brochure to explain his patriotic stance to the public: "The sudden and simultaneous outburst of patriotism . . . when the flag of the country was insulted and the Government defied and betrayed, found no more hearty response among any class of citizen than the Artists. . . ."[4] Church produced a chromolithograph of *Our Banner in the Sky*, which quickly became a best seller in the North (fig. 9).

Church and his party arrived in Jamaica on May 1 on the steamer *Montezuma*, first staying at the suburban villa of Mr. Derbyshire, in the hamlet of Bellevue, five miles from Kingston, just as the rainy season began.[5] The artist and his wife dealt with their sorrow, each in different ways, as Robbins noted in one of the many letters he sent to his mother during his island sojourn: "Poor Mr. & Mrs. Church I feel very sorry for them.

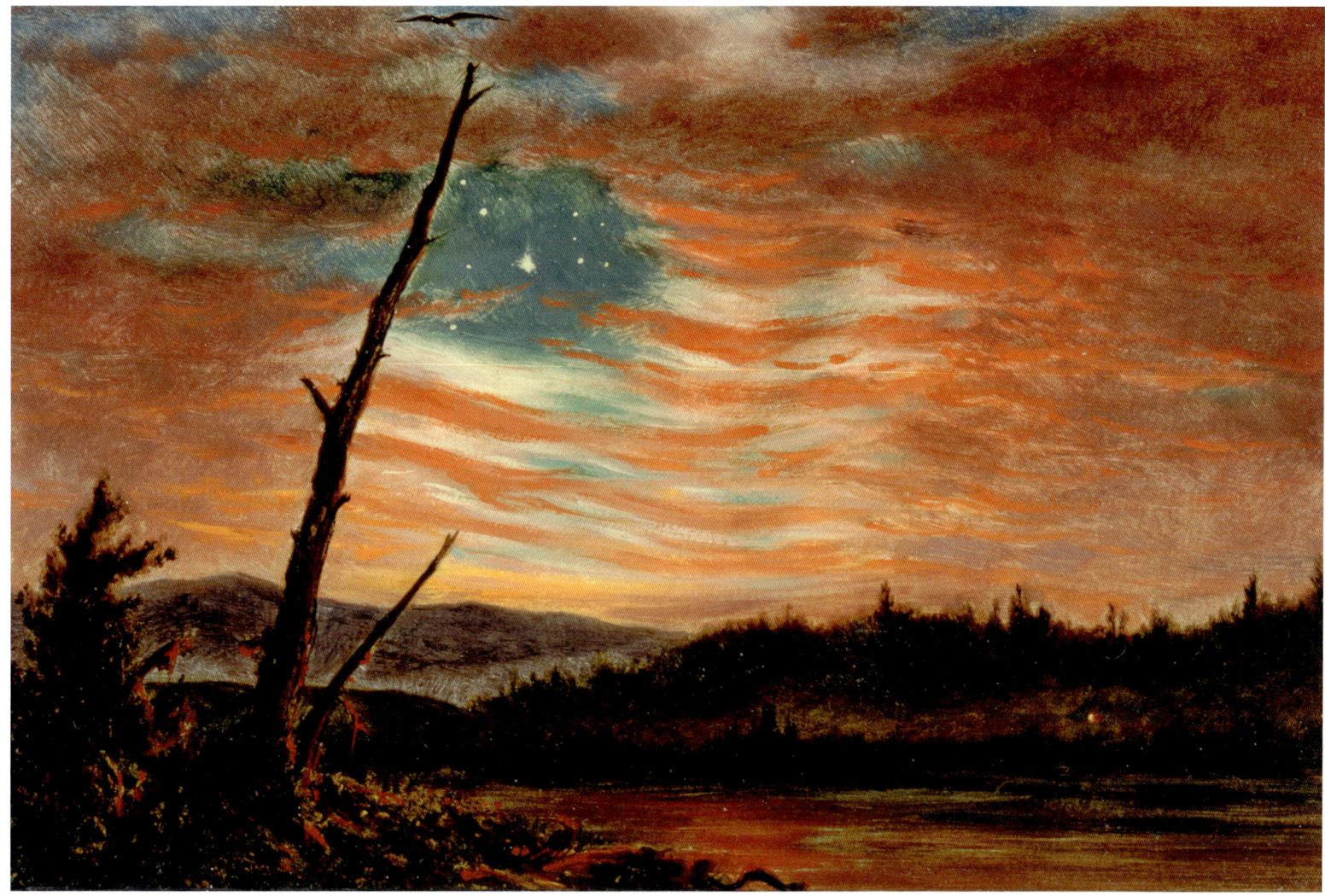

Fig. 9. Chromolithograph, published by
Goupil and Co., 1861, oil over chromolithograph, after Frederic Edwin Church,
Our Banner in the Sky, April–May 1861,
7⁹⁄₁₆ × 11⅜ in., OL.1976.29

She is often very sad & speaks to Sarah about her children. He is very singular about that—never likes to speak of his feelings. . . . He works away as if for dear life—& seems to be trying to forget his trouble by always keeping himself occupied."[6] After several months, they settled at Galloway Hill, as the guests of Mr. Charles Fyffe, who was the curate at the Parish Church at Port Royal. The property was adjacent to Governor Edward John Eyre's renowned summer residence, Flamstead, where the Churches were likely included in the governor's frequent parties.[7]

In a frenzy of activity, the artist directed his attention to the topography, botany, and meteorology of the tropical landscape, producing one of his greatest series of plein air oil sketches (fig. 10).[8] Tuckerman noted the diversity of subjects that resulted:

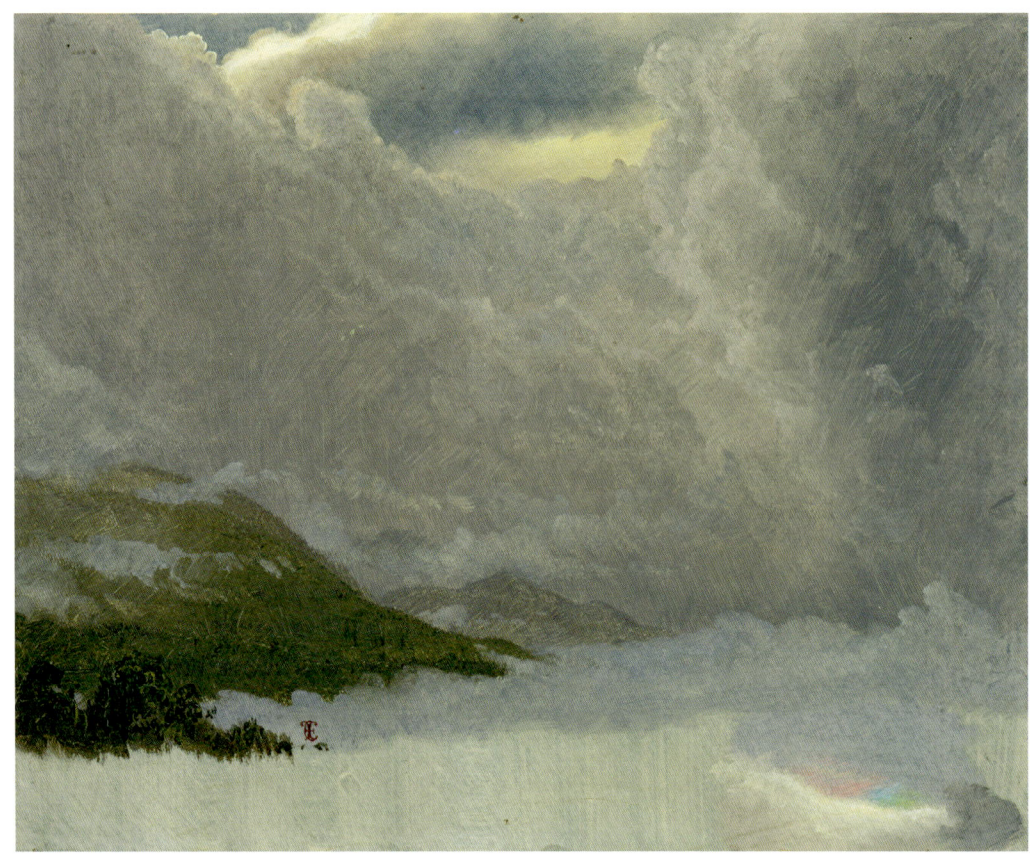

Fig. 10. Frederic Edwin Church, *Storm in the Blue Mountains, Jamaica*, August 1865, oil on academy board, 10 × 12 1/16 in., OL.1976.16

The studies which he brought home . . . are admirable effects of sunset, storm, and mist, caught in all their evanescent but characteristic phases; the mountain shapes, gorges, plateaus, lines of coast, and outlines of hills; besides these general features, there are minute and elaborate studies of vegetation—the palms, ferns, canebrakes, flowers, grasses, and lizards; in a word, all the materials of a tropical insular landscape, with every local trait carefully noted.[9]

As a close observer of nature, Church produced a number of independent sketches of Jamaica and, for the first time, began signing his studies.[10] In such oil studies as *Tropical Vines and Trees, Jamaica*, May to July 1865 (fig. 11), executed in an unusual vertical format, and the ink drawing *Coconut Palms, Kingston, Jamaica*, July 7, 1865 (fig. 12), the artist recorded the lush botanical subjects he encountered. He also executed a drawing, *Scenery near Fern Walk, Jamaica*, September 1865 (fig. 13), and an oil study entitled *Fern Walk, Jamaica*, July 1865 (fig. 14), that he later framed to hang at Olana, showing a winding path through the tall ferns that were a highlight of the island scenery and that captured the fancy of his wife. In the company of Sarah Hitchcock,[11] Isabel developed

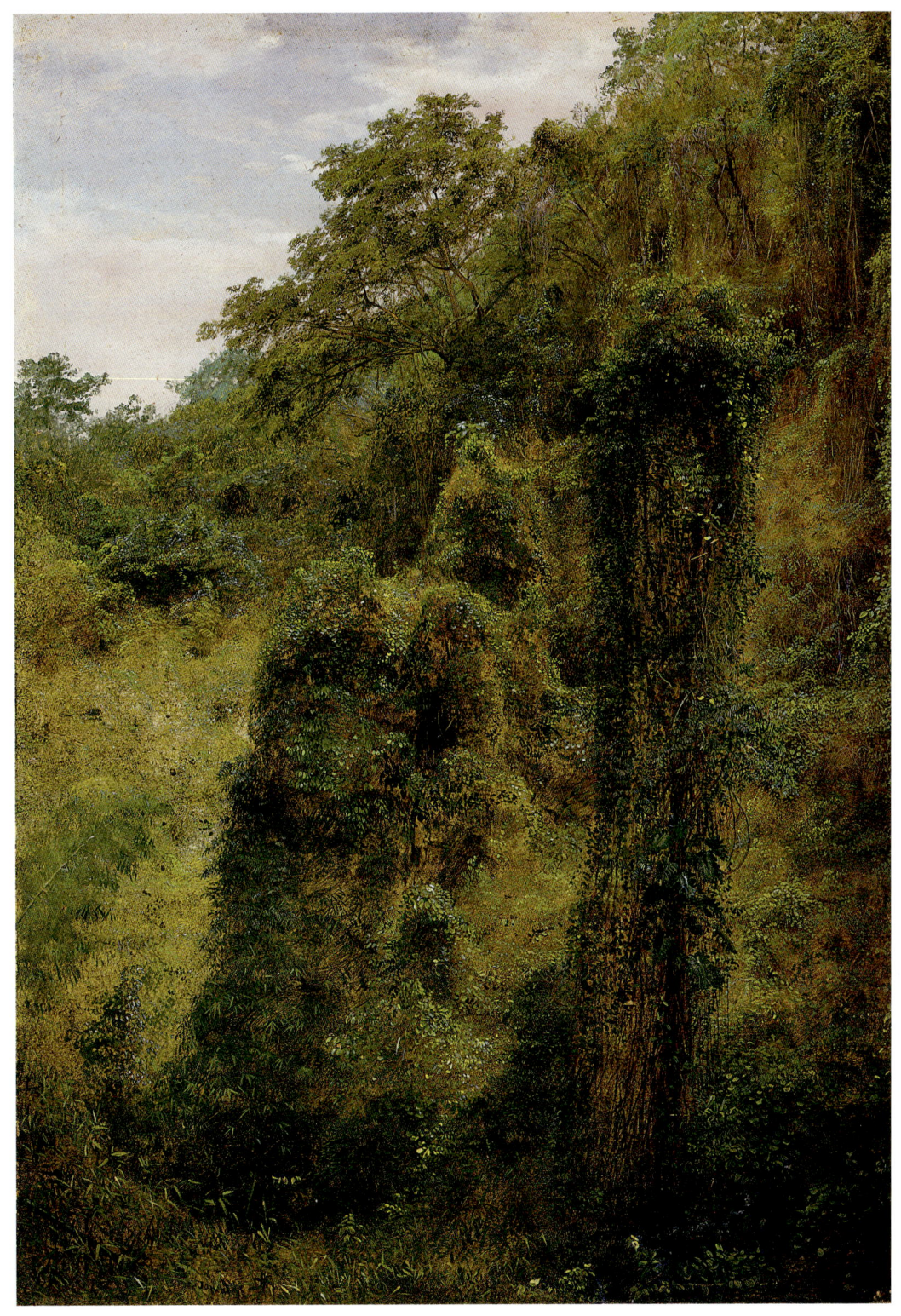

Fig. 11. Frederic Edwin Church, *Tropical Vines and Trees, Jamaica*, c. May–July 1865, oil on paper mounted on wood, 18⅛ × 12½ in., OL.1980.1948

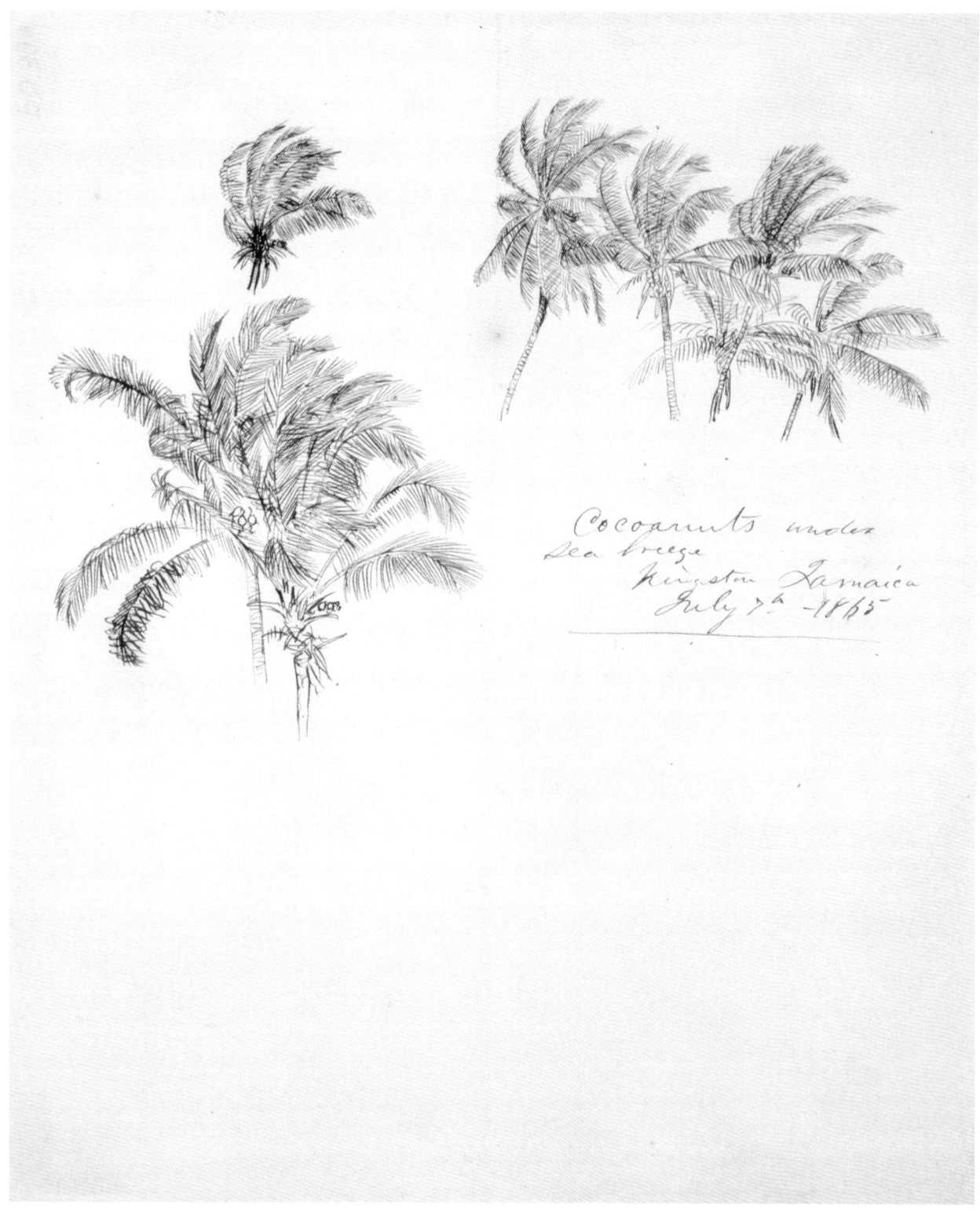

Cocoanuts under
Sea breeze
Kingston Jamaica
July 7th -1865

Fig. 12. Frederic Edwin Church, *Coconut Palms, Kingston, Jamaica*, July 7, 1865, ink on paper, 9⅞ × 7⅞ in., OL.1977.119

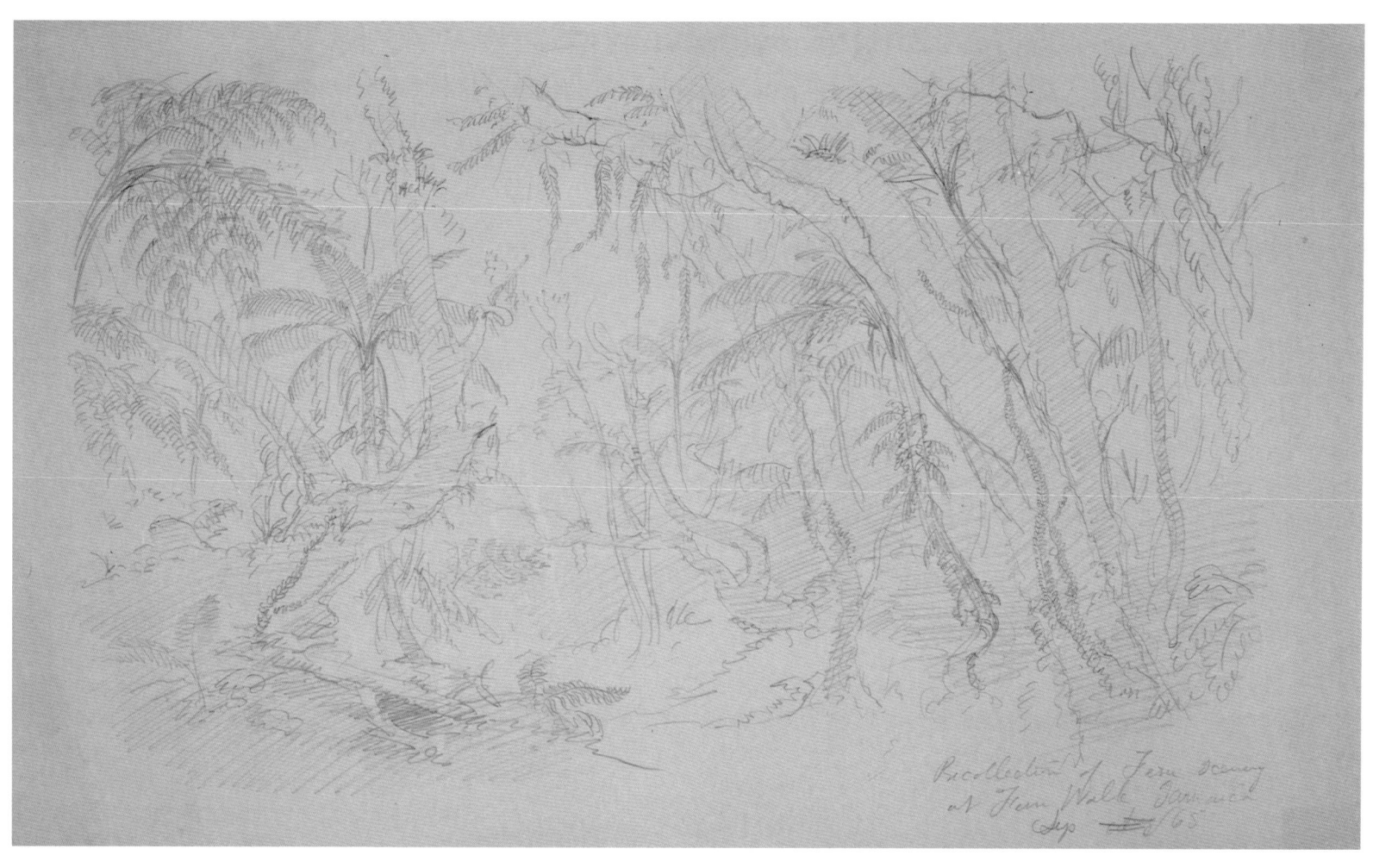

Fig. 13. Frederic Edwin Church, *Scenery near Fern Walk*, *Jamaica*, September 1865, graphite on light blue-green paper, 10¾ × 17⅜ in., OL.1977.101

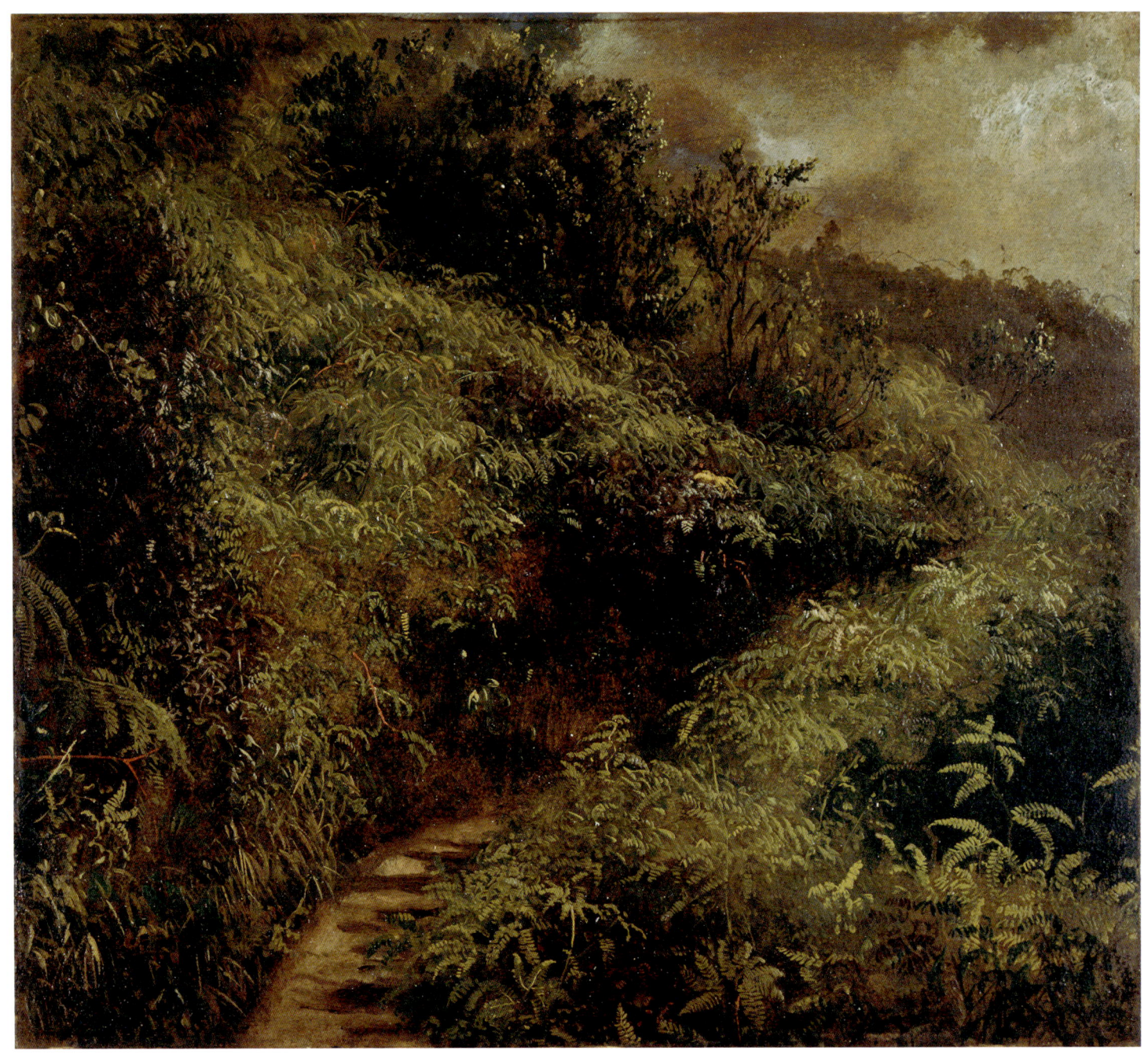

Fig. 14. Frederic Edwin Church, *Fern Walk, Jamaica*, July 1865, oil on paper mounted on canvas, 12¼ × 13¼ in., OL.1981.73

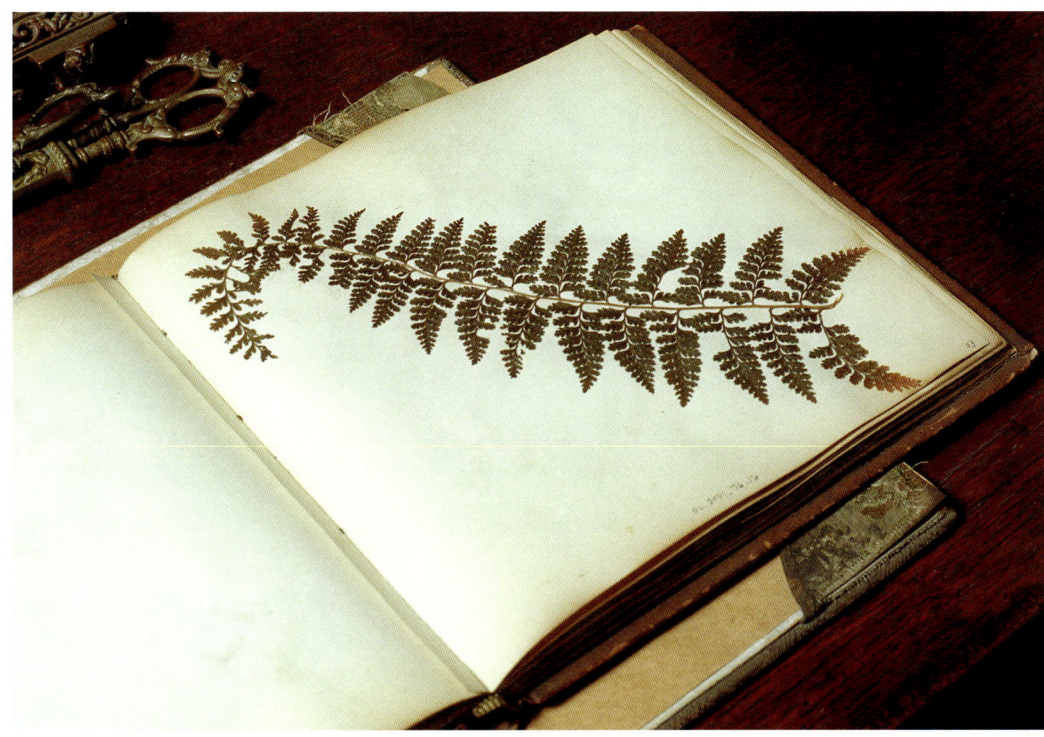

Fig. 15. Isabel Carnes Church, *Pressed Fern in an Herbarium*, OL.2001.76, Image Courtesy Nicholas Whitman, 2003, nwphoto.com

a passion for ferns, as Frederic reported: "Mrs. Church is fascinated with the occupation of fern collecting and has already an enormous collection."[12] The Churches returned with the fern collection, including live specimens and pressed ferns, which remain at Olana (fig. 15), and also added to their library *The Fern Garden* (1869) by Shirley Hibberd.[13] They planted a fern bed at Olana, located below the carriage turn on the north side of the house (fig. 16), and placed potted ferns in their dining room (fig. 17).

With the intention of completing the far-advanced canvas *Rainy Season in the Tropics* (fig. 18), which was sitting on his easel in New York, at the Tenth Street Studio Building (fig. 19), Church focused on executing additional sketches for its final composition. But perhaps foremost on his mind, as he roamed the island on horseback, traversing the island's interior, was his search for a suitable subject for the commission he had received from his close friend Elizabeth Hart Jarvis Colt for a major work that would become the centerpiece of her private picture gallery in Hartford, Connecticut. His efforts resulted in his most important Jamaican landscape, *The Vale of St. Thomas, Jamaica*, 1867 (fig. 1).

The close familial ties between the Church and the Colt and Jarvis families of Hartford went back several generations. Elizabeth Colt (1826–1905), like her contemporary Frederic Church, had suffered the deaths of an infant son and daughter, as well as that of another daughter only six months after the death of her husband, Samuel Colt. At midcentury, Samuel Colt (1814–1862) was internationally famous as an inventor,

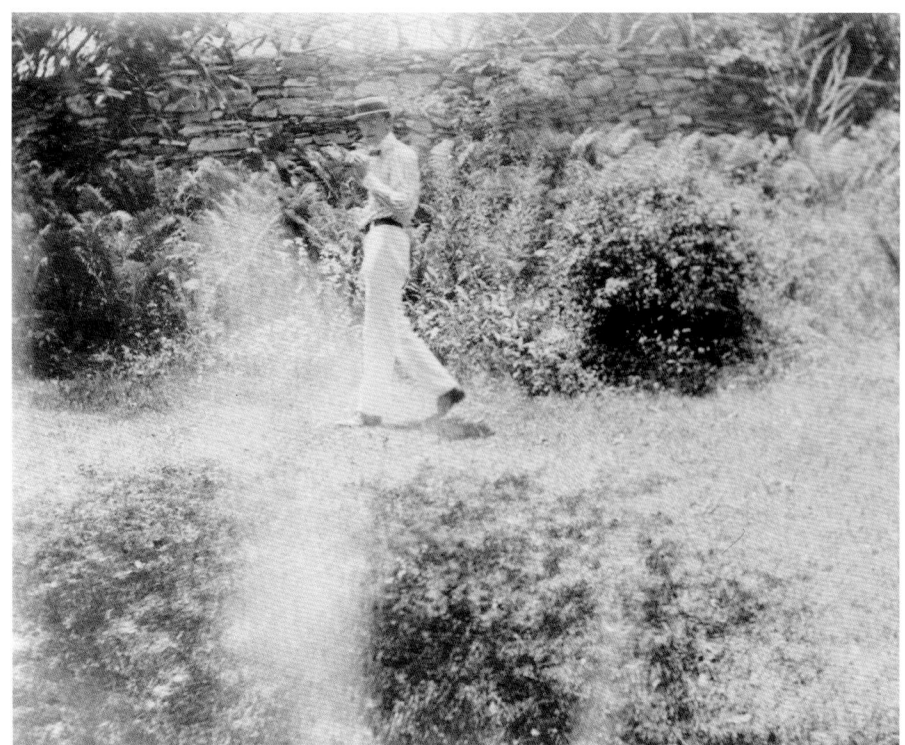

Fig. 16. Unknown photographer, *Louis Church Walking by the Fern Bed, North of the Main House at Olana*, c. 1885–1914, photograph, 4 × 5 in., OL.1986.378.6.D

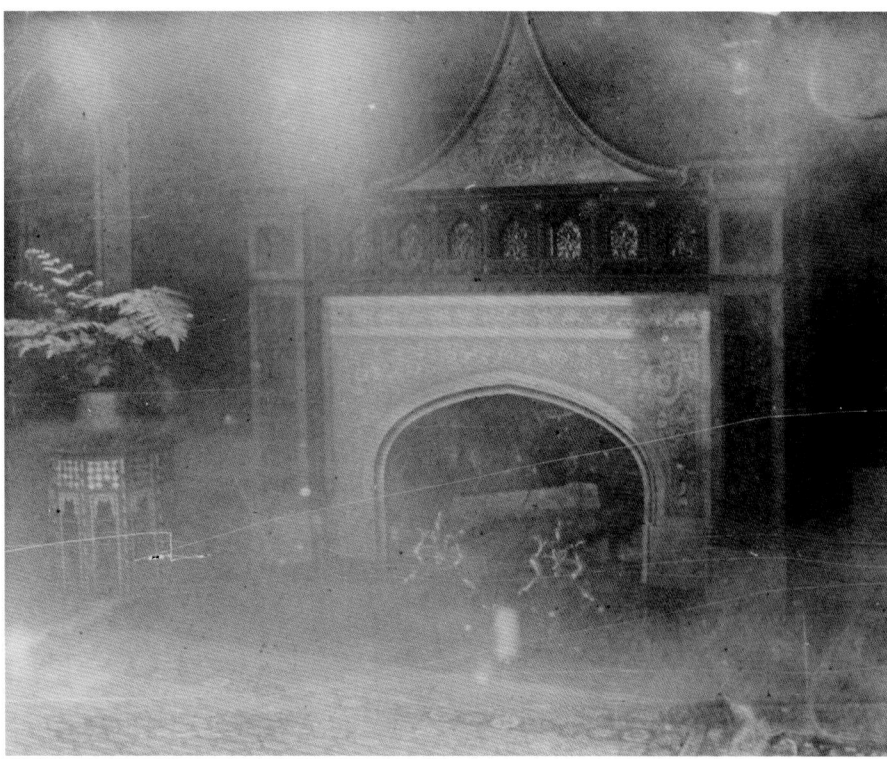

Fig. 17. Unknown photographer, *Potted Fern on Tabouret Table in the Dining Room at Olana*, c. 1885–1914, photograph, 3⅝ × 4⅝ in., OL.1986.378.21.B

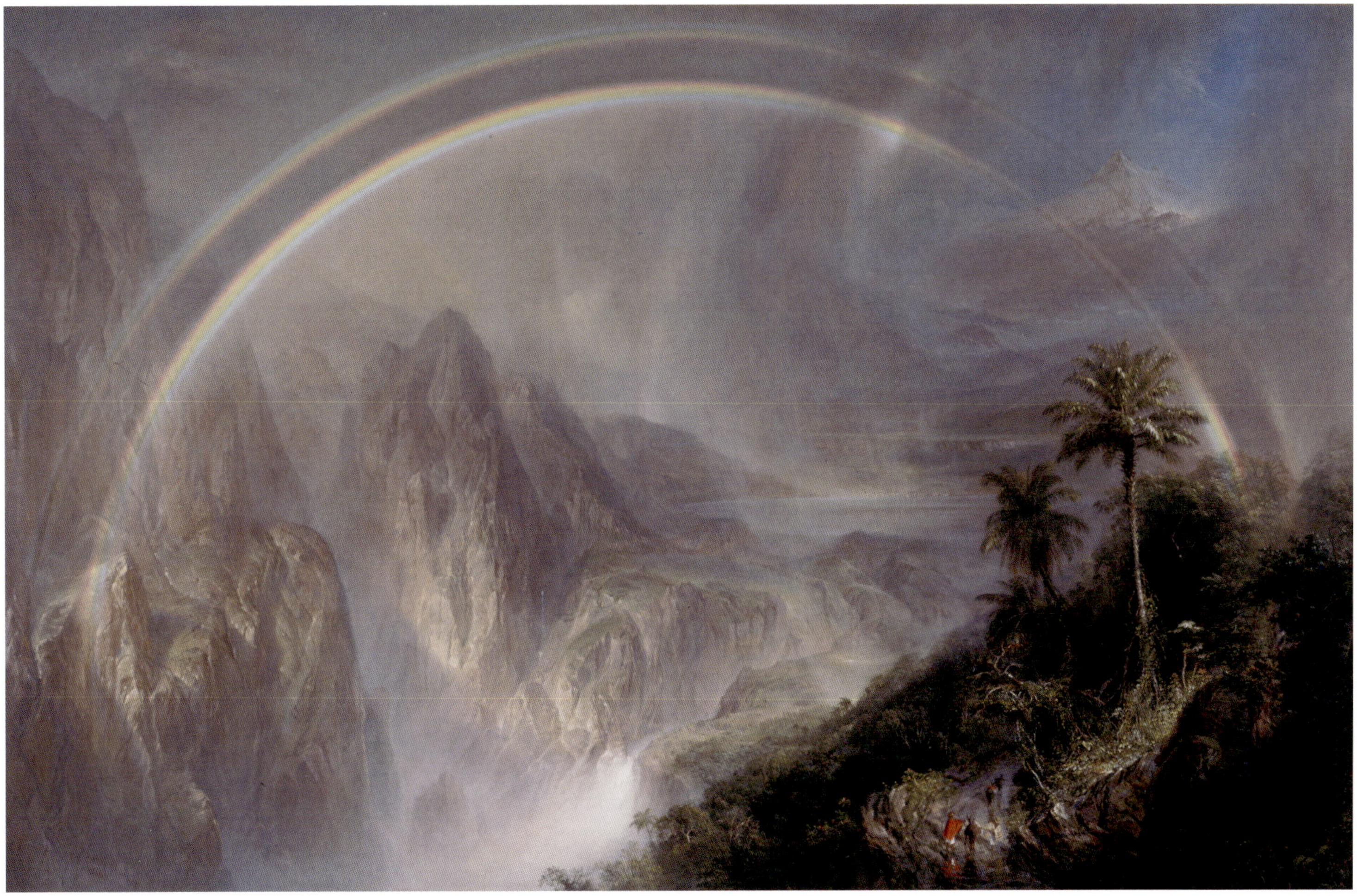

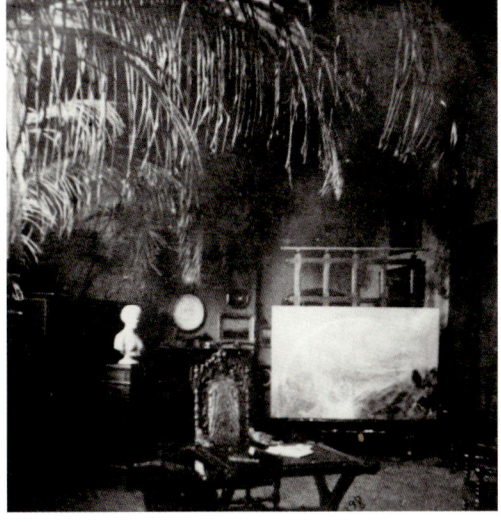

Fig. 18. Frederic Edwin Church, *Rainy Season in the Tropics*, 1866, oil on canvas, 56¼ × 84¼ in., Fine Arts Museums of San Francisco, Museum Purchase, Mildred Anna Williams Collection, 1970.9

Fig. 19. S. Beer, *"Rainy Season in the Tropics" on View in Frederic Church's Tenth Street Studio, New York, New York*, c. 1866, stereograph, 3¼ × 6¾ in., OL.1985.815

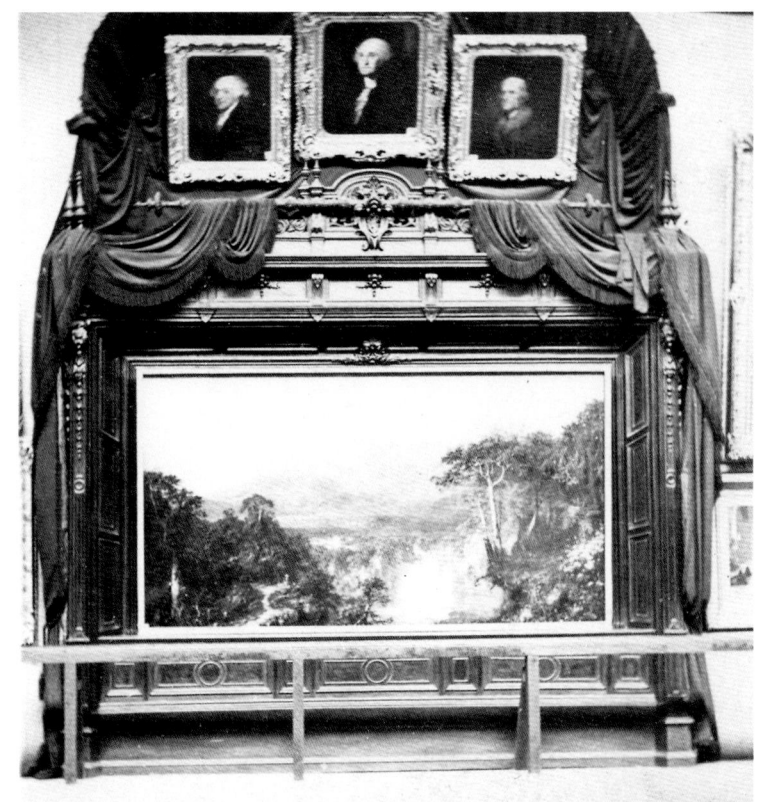

Fig. 20. Unknown photographer, *"The Heart of the Andes" by Frederic Edwin Church as Exhibited at the Metropolitan Sanitary Fair*, 1864, stereograph, Collection of The New-York Historical Society, New-York Historical Society Manuscripts Collection, negative number 61263

manufacturer, and purveyor of firearms. In Hartford, he constructed the largest private armory in the world, on a two-hundred-acre stretch of land along the Connecticut River. The couple built Armsmear, an Italianate villa overlooking the Colt armory, which was among the most elaborate residences in America. As one of the wealthiest women in the country, with a controlling interest in her deceased husband's Colt arms manufactory, Mrs. Colt intended to create a picture gallery that would rival any in the country.[14]

Church, whose parents and sister were close friends and neighbors of Elizabeth Colt, served as her chief adviser in the planning and design of the gallery and the acquisition of suitable works. The inspiration for the idea may have arisen from Elizabeth's participation in the 1864 New York Metropolitan Sanitary Fair, a relief effort to raise funds for medical services for the Union army. An abolitionist sympathizer and a staunch supporter of the Union cause, Elizabeth hosted the Hartford Table, where she sold all of the tea cakes she had made along with all the Colt revolvers on display.[15] She found time to visit the art gallery, the most popular of the many exhibits at the Sanitary Fair. Organized by the Committee on the Fine Arts, composed of New York's cultural leaders, including Frederic Church, the gallery offered a survey of taste at the time. The most popular works were by Americans, the most acclaimed being Church's *Niagara*, *The Heart of the Andes*

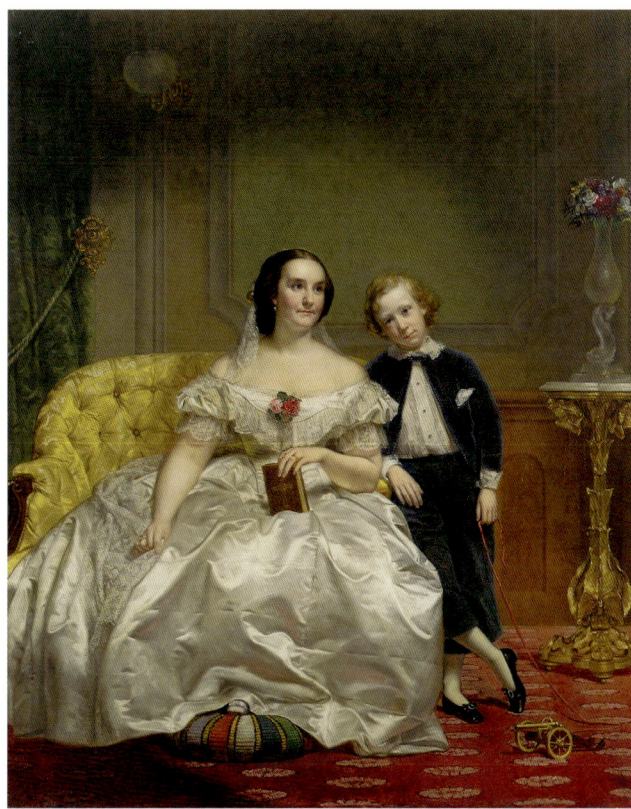

Fig. 21. Charles Loring Elliott, *Mrs. Elizabeth Hart Jarvis Colt and Her Son Caldwell*, 1865, oil on canvas, 84 × 66 in., Wadsworth Atheneum Museum of Art, Hartford, Conn., Bequest of Elizabeth Hart Jarvis Colt, 1905.9

(fig. 7), lent by real estate tycoon William T. Blodgett, and *Twilight in the Wilderness* (fig. 8), lent by railroad magnate John Taylor Johnston.[16] These works, painted shortly before the opening salvo of the Civil War, conveyed strong nationalistic overtones. *The Heart of the Andes* was placed in a massive architectural frame (as a window into the tropical landscape), set off with lavish drapes, and surmounted by the portraits of three American presidents (fig. 20), while *Twilight in the Wilderness* presaged an American apocalypse with the approach of the Civil War.[17]

Impressed by the art gallery and strongly influenced by the arrangement itself, Elizabeth conceived an ambitious plan for her own picture gallery the following year. With the assistance of Church, she commissioned the leading New York portrait painter Charles Loring Elliott to paint a grand-scale portrait of herself (fig. 21) and a posthumous memorial portrait of her husband. After Colt's death, Elizabeth maintained close control over the factory, and she had some bearing on the outcome of the Civil War by supplying only the Union army with guns.[18]

After an arduous journey across Jamaica by train, on horseback, and on foot, Church and Robbins finally laid eyes on the scene that would inspire Mrs. Colt's painting. Robbins provided a description of that moment:

A week ago last Tuesday, Mr. Church and I went off on an exploring expedition toward the Northern side of the island. . . . We soon began the ascent of Monte Diablo—a wild & pretty high mountain. Here the mountains however lofty seem to be covered with foliage, to the very summits— Reaching the highest elevation we had one of the sweetest & finest views I have yet seen on the island— In the far distance was a long blue range of Blue hills and near the thickly wooded hills and down the valleys—great mosses & clouds of fogs wh[ich] seemed like lakes whilst here & there above it peeped out some tall palms.—

It was a sight never to be forgotten—so beautiful and grand— We overlooked the Parish of "St Thomas in the Vale" wh[ich] is one of the sweetest of them all— We remained sometime enjoying the view.[19]

Church produced copious oil studies from this vantage point, a large number of them in preparation for the painting that would become *The Vale of St. Thomas, Jamaica*

Fig. 22. Frederic Edwin Church, *Scene in the Blue Mountains, Jamaica*, August 1865, oil on paper mounted on academy board, 10⅝ × 17¾ in., OL.1981.69

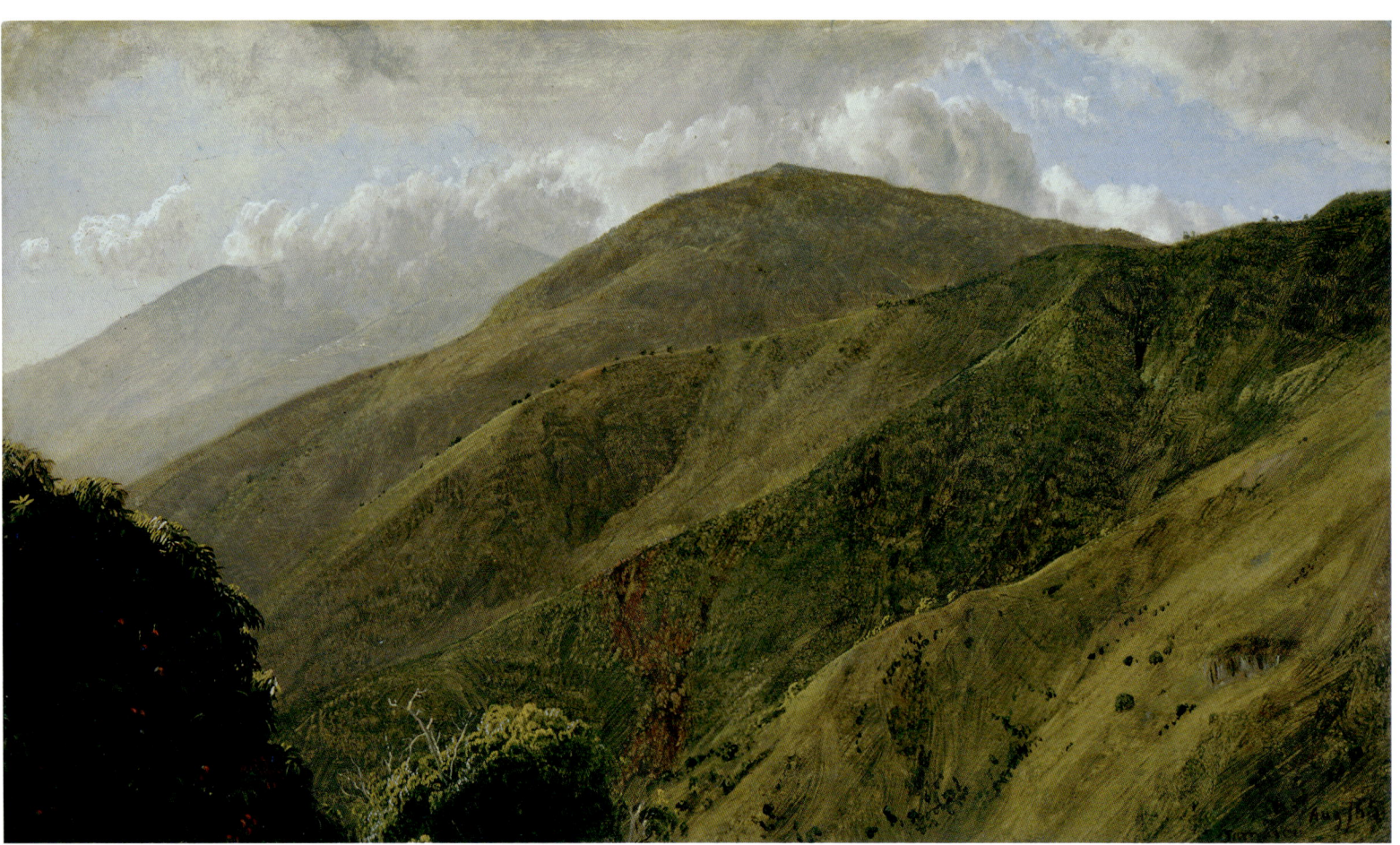

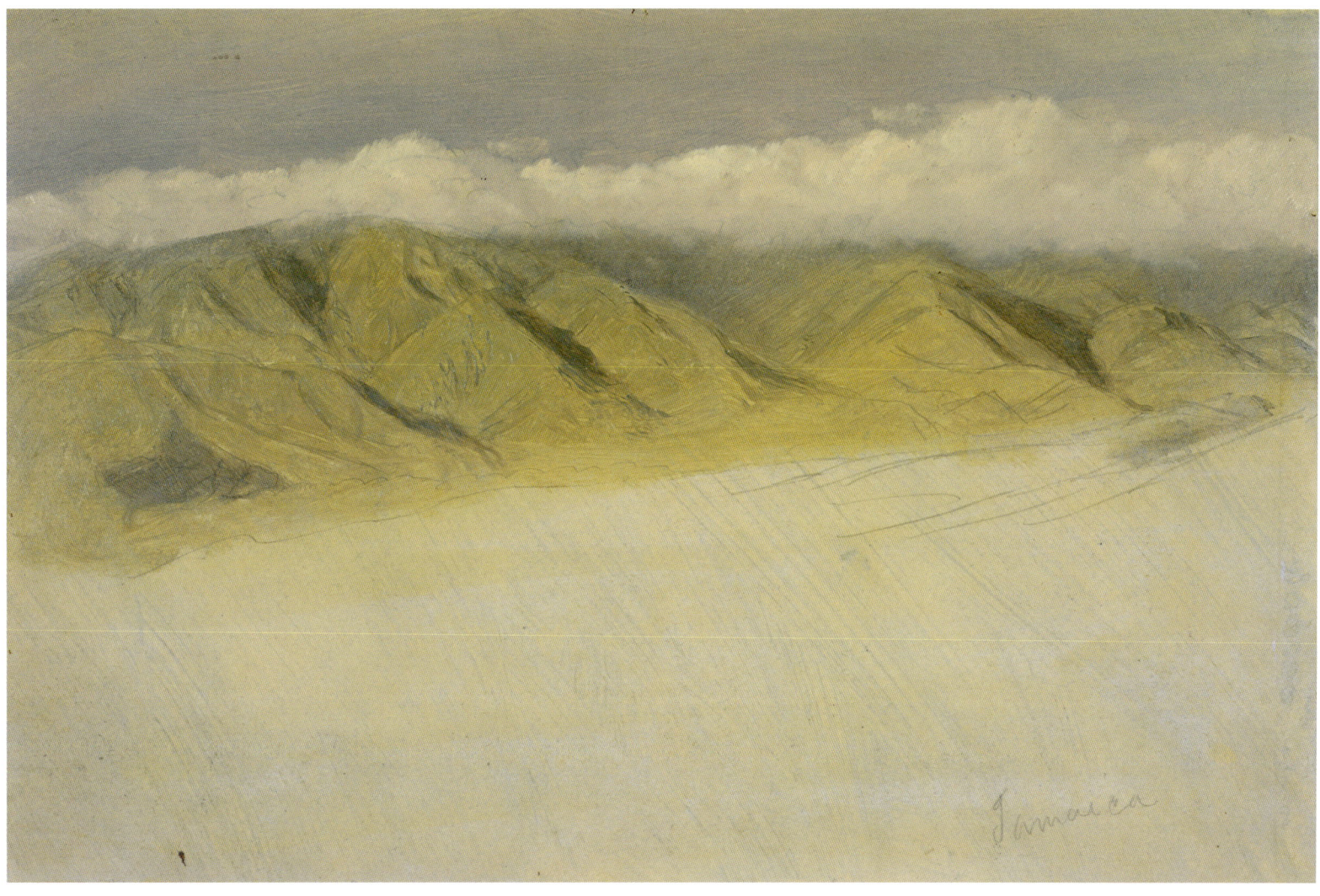

(many of these are in the collection of the Cooper-Hewitt, National Design Museum, New York, as well as at Olana). In such exquisite oil studies as *Scene in the Blue Mountains, Jamaica* (fig. 22), *Ridges in the Blue Mountains, Jamaica* (fig. 2), *Blue Mountains, Jamaica* (fig. 23), *Clouds in the Blue Mountains, Jamaica* (fig. 24), *Storm in the Blue Mountains, Jamaica* (fig. 10), and *In the Blue Mountains, Jamaica* (fig. 25), Church explored the spectacular rainstorms that crossed the valley, the brilliant sunsets, the rich colors of the Blue Mountains, and the lush vegetation. In his oil studies, he also indicated drought conditions (fig. 2), which were severe that summer and caused tension on the island, and which he later acknowledged in a letter to Theodore Cole, the manager of Church's Hudson Valley farm and the son of his mentor Thomas Cole.[20]

Fig. 23. Frederic Edwin Church, *Blue Mountains, Jamaica*, c. July–August 1865, oil and graphite on paper, 8⅟₁₆ × 12 in., OL.1976.2

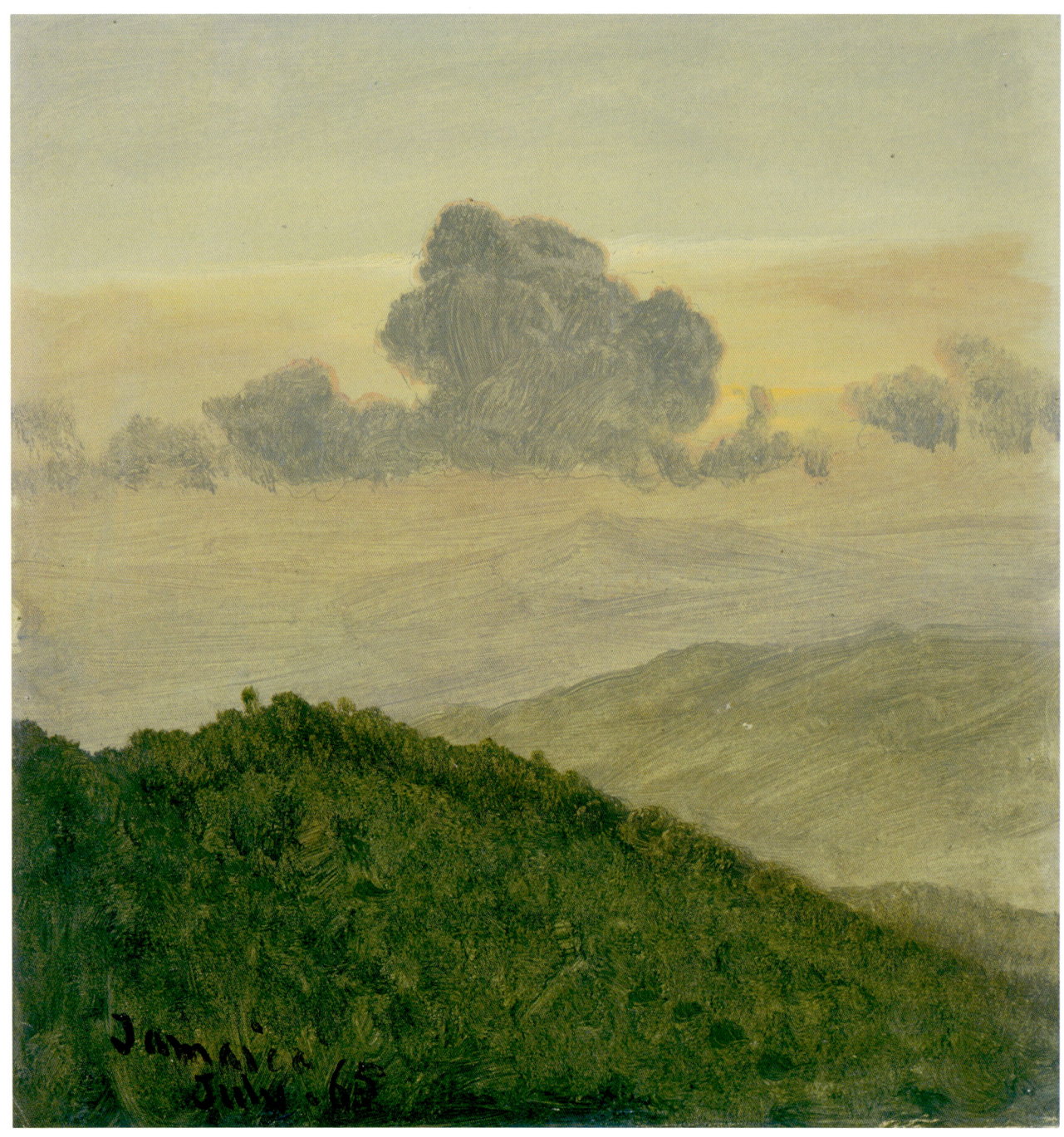

Fig. 24. Frederic Edwin Church, *Clouds in the Blue Mountains, Jamaica*, July 1865, oil on paper mounted on academy board, 11⅛ × 10¼ in., OL.1976.15

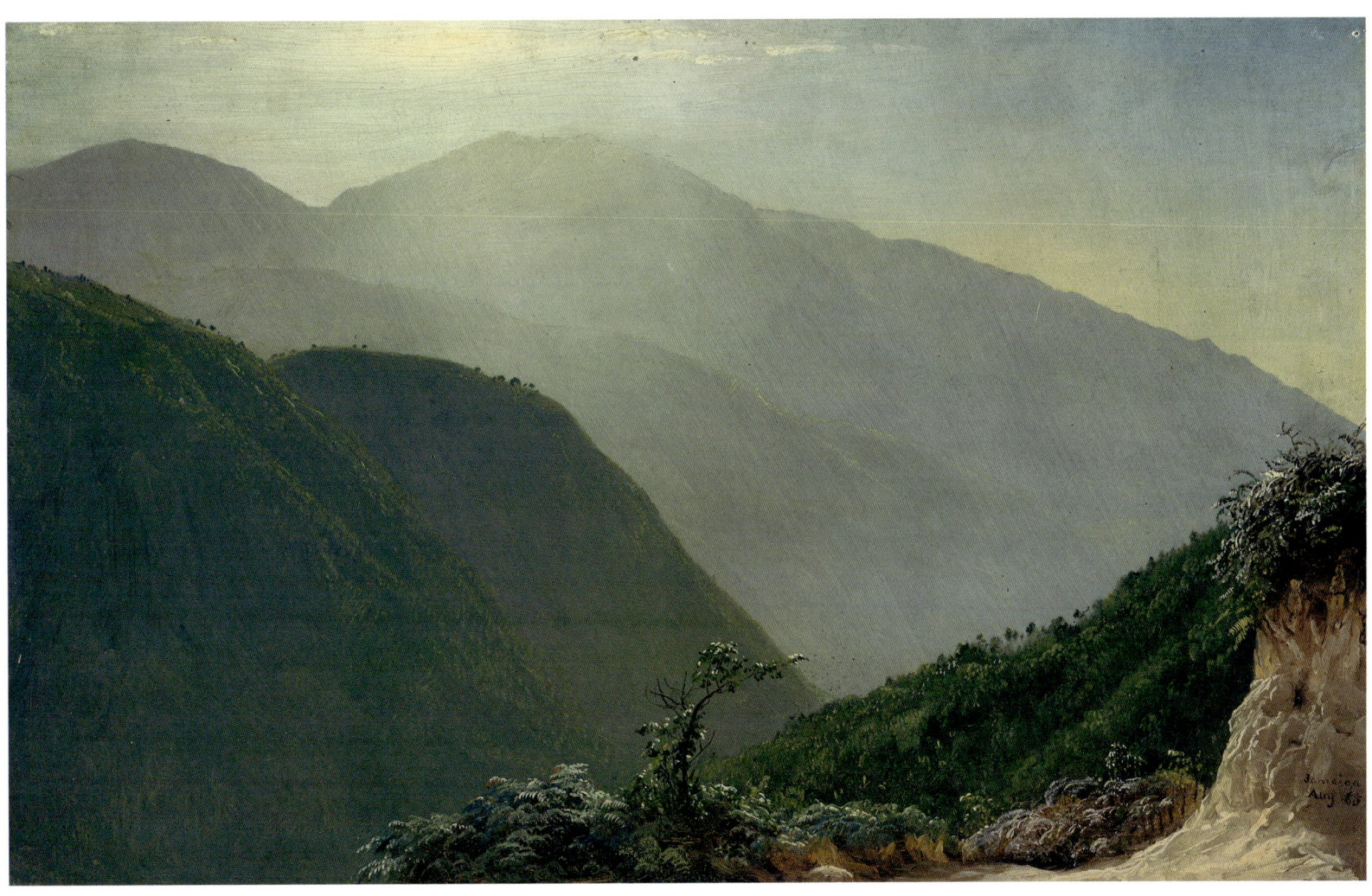

Fig. 25. Frederic Edwin Church, *In the Blue Mountains, Jamaica*, August 1865, oil on paperboard, 11¼ × 17⅞ in., Cooper-Hewitt, National Design Museum, New York, Smithsonian Institution, Gift of Louis P. Church, 1917-4-419, Photograph: Scott Hyde

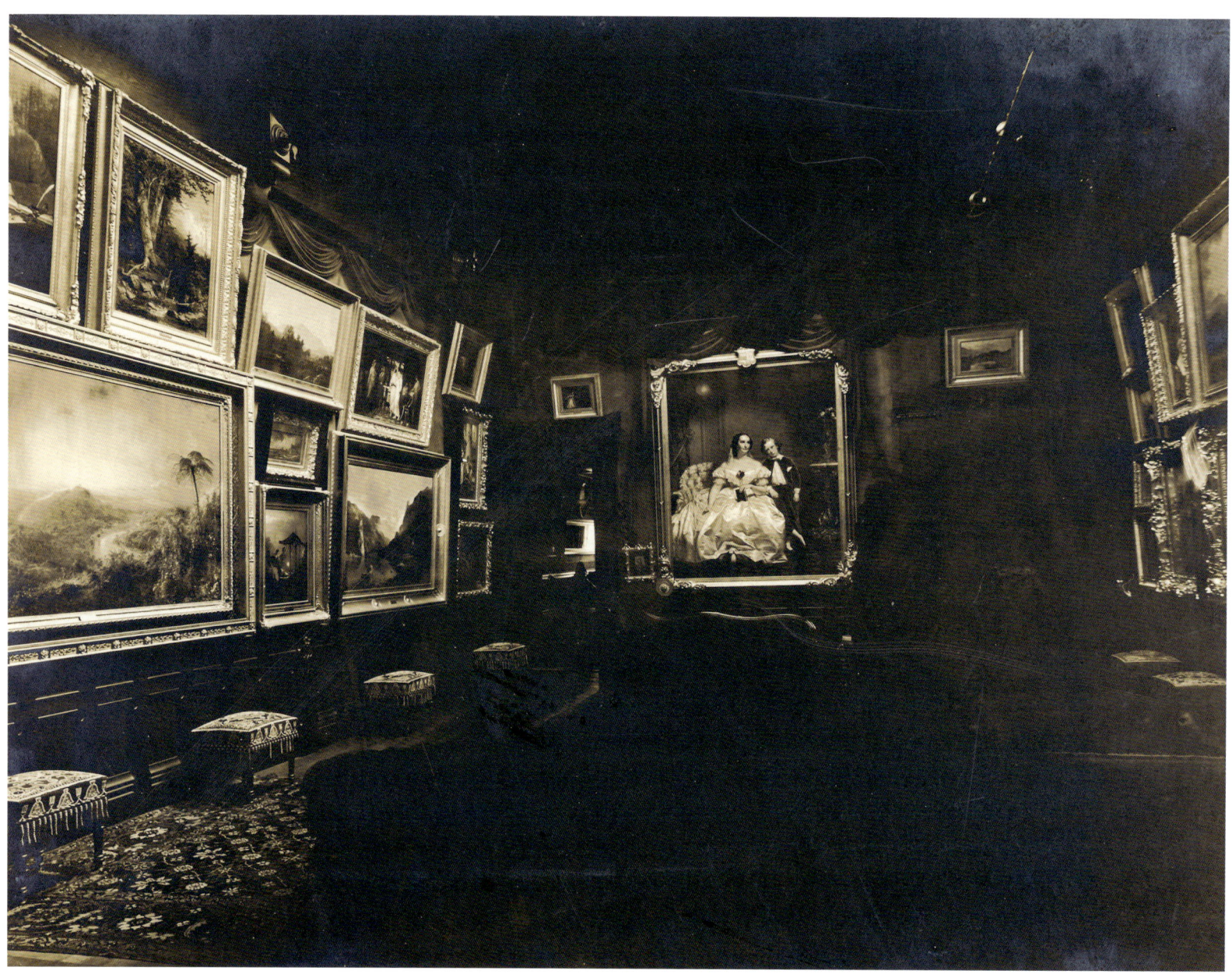

Fig. 26. Unknown photographer, *South View of Elizabeth Colt's Picture Gallery on the Second Floor of Armsmear*, 1880, photograph, Wadsworth Atheneum Museum of Art, Hartford, Conn., Archives

Shortly after the Churches departed for home in September, the unrest that had been building up on the island over the summer—the culmination of grievances resulting from the legacy of slavery—led to the worst violence Jamaica had experienced in decades. Conflict broke out between Jamaican blacks, who, although free since 1834, were left with no rights and very little means for making a living, and British colonials on October 11, beginning at Morant Bay in St. Thomas-in-the-East, on the island's eastern end. Governor Eyre declared martial law in the eastern parishes and brutally crushed the uprising. The event quickly escalated into a bloody suppression described at the time as a "wholesale and indiscriminate massacre" of Jamaicans.[21] A court-martial of Governor Eyre followed, reported in newspapers from New York to London. The trial, which lasted for three years, attracted the advocacy of Charles Darwin and Charles Lyell, among others, who wanted Eyre brought to justice, and who clashed with members of the Eyre Defense Committee, which included John Ruskin and Thomas Carlyle.[22] It is hard not to see *The Vale of St. Thomas, Jamaica* (fig. 1), which depicts the very region involved in the incidents, as relating to the series of paintings by Church that responded to the great conflict of the Civil War in the United States and the issue of slavery.[23] The work, completed as the Civil War was coming to a close, may have reflected the mood of relief at the end of hostilities. In addition, with the knowledge that the legacy of slavery on the island of Jamaica continued to cause conflict thirty years after emancipation, Church may have wished that this work serve as a warning for Americans that the end of the Civil War was only a beginning for the United States. Finally, he knew that Elizabeth Colt—a supporter of the Union and a woman who had taken strong positions as an abolitionist—would make it the centerpiece of her gallery (fig. 26).

After the Churches' return in September, the artist's spirits were renewed by the improved national mood following the end of the war, as well as by the birth of a son in September 1866. Mrs. Colt corresponded with Church that fall concerning progress on the construction of her "Picture Gallery," concluding, "I want very much to see your picture for me & am sure it will be a never ending delight."[24] Church had begun the painting in 1866 and was still working on it later the following year.[25]

In 1866, the second floor of Armsmear was torn up to accommodate skylights as construction began on the gallery. Colt hired the renowned New York architect William Morris Hunt, who had served on the Metropolitan Sanitary Fair Committee on the Fine Arts and had designed the Tenth Street Studio Building, which provided work spaces for Church and many other leading Hudson River School painters, to oversee the project. Church advised Colt on lighting, furnishings, and wall construction, and he provided access to his frame maker. He assured her, "I believe that you will have the most charming gallery in the country—I am anxious to see it."[26]

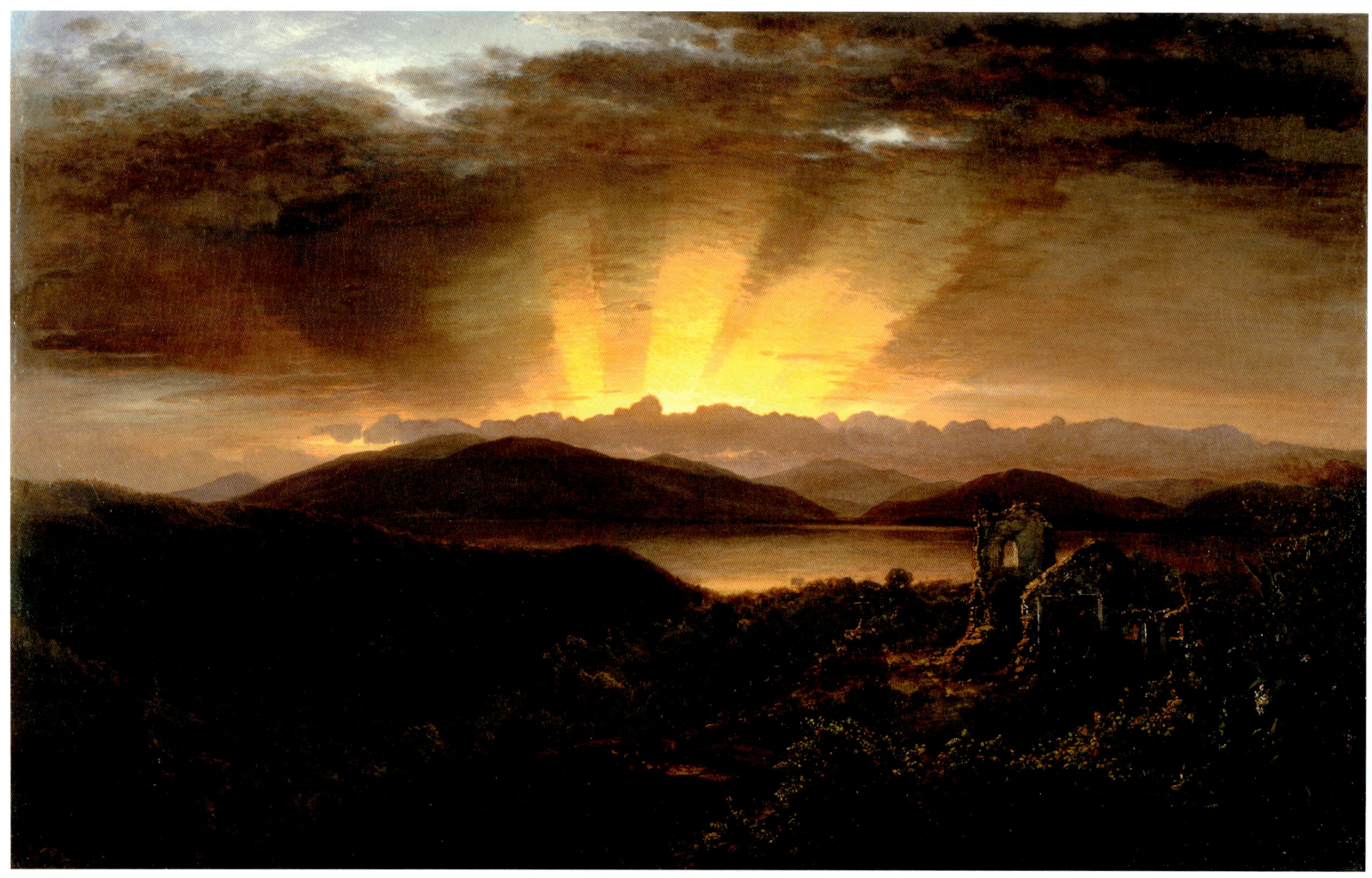

Fig. 27. Frederic Edwin Church, *The After Glow,*
November 1867, oil on canvas, 31¼ × 48¾ in.,
OL.1981.48

For his composition, Church chose a site-specific representation of the island's
interior as viewed from an elevation on Mount Diablo looking across the Valley of
St. Thomas toward the Blue Mountains. Aware that the painting would serve as the
focal point of the gallery, which Mrs. Colt intended as a memorial to her deceased husband, Church took care to evoke a spiritual meaning in his tropical landscape. As he
explained in detail in a letter to Elizabeth Colt, he chose to depict the moment of a
"passing shower of tropical character . . . the sun is struggling . . . subdued by the veil of
mist and rain . . . the sun is so brilliantly illuminated with its clear unobscured rays that
it shines (or I wish it to) with almost dazzling light."[27] The brilliant light of the setting
sun struggles to emerge from behind a passing rain cloud, creating a swirling vortex of
light and atmosphere reminiscent of the canvases of Joseph Mallord William Turner. In
this idealized landscape, a tiny monastery placed high above the horizon, overlooking

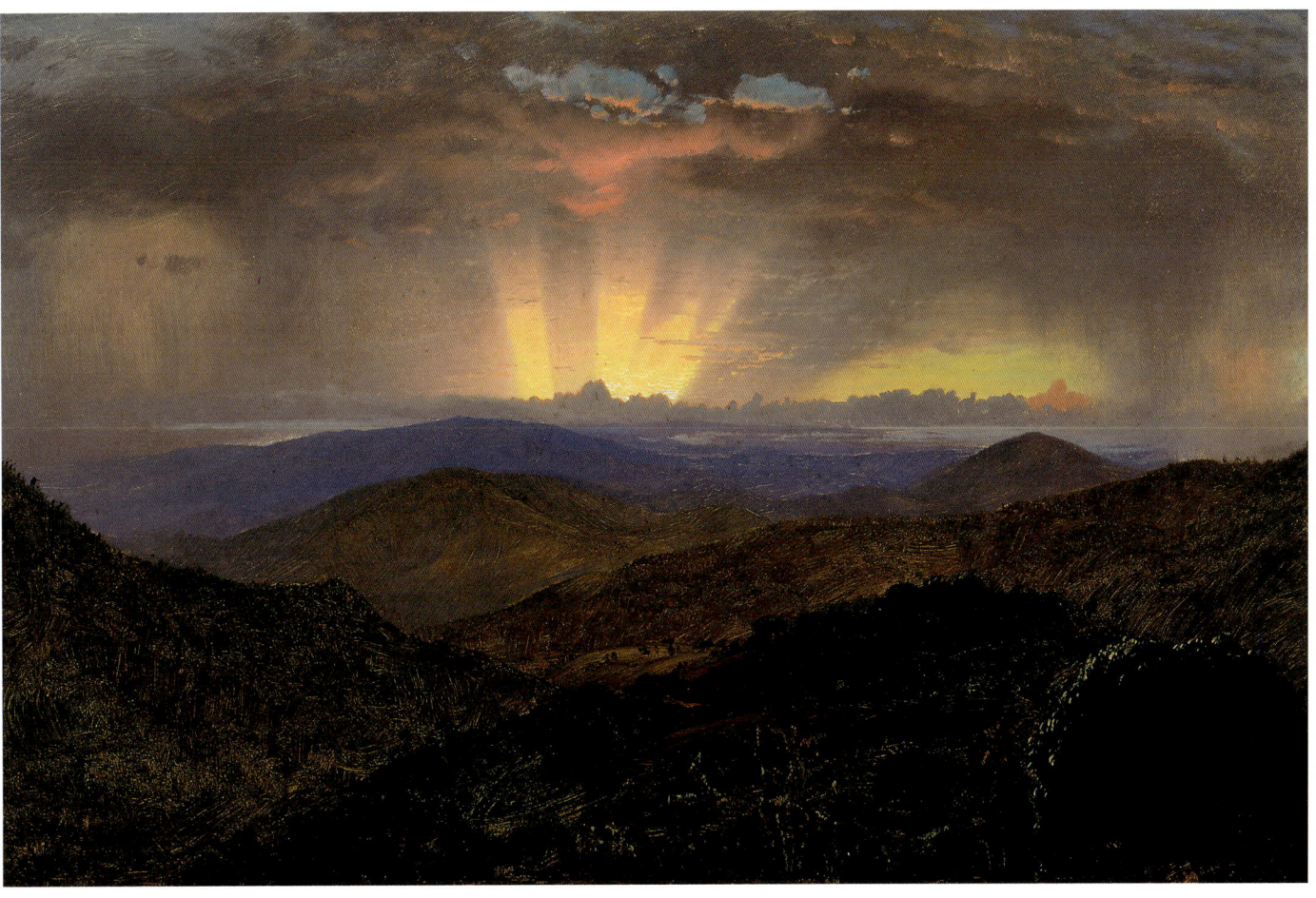

the river, symbolizes divine presence in the tropics. Church completed the canvas by designing an elaborate gilt shadow-box frame to surround it. He also sent a large "tree fern" to Mrs. Colt to be placed alongside the painting for greater effect.[28]

Although Church finished the painting in 1867, he left with his family on an eighteen-month trip to Europe and the Middle East in the fall of that year. Thus, Mrs. Colt may not actually have received the painting until after its public exhibition, from April 4 to the end of May 1870 at the Goupil Gallery in New York, where it was titled simply *Jamaica*.[29] Church "retouched" the picture for the exhibition, as was his habit.[30] The work received favorable notice; one critic praised the painting by noting it "combined the effect of storm and sunshine . . . with the most vivid and startling power."[31]

Church made one additional large canvas related to his trip to Jamaica, entitled *The After Glow* (fig. 27). He based it on his studies of a spectacular sunset that he had seen in July 1865. One of these, *Sunset, Jamaica* (fig. 28), documented the intense yellow rays that Church witnessed, and which carried a strong spiritual significance for the artist.[32]

Fig. 28. Frederic Edwin Church, *Sunset, Jamaica*, July 1865, oil on paper mounted on canvas, 12⅛ × 18⅛ in., OL.1981.26

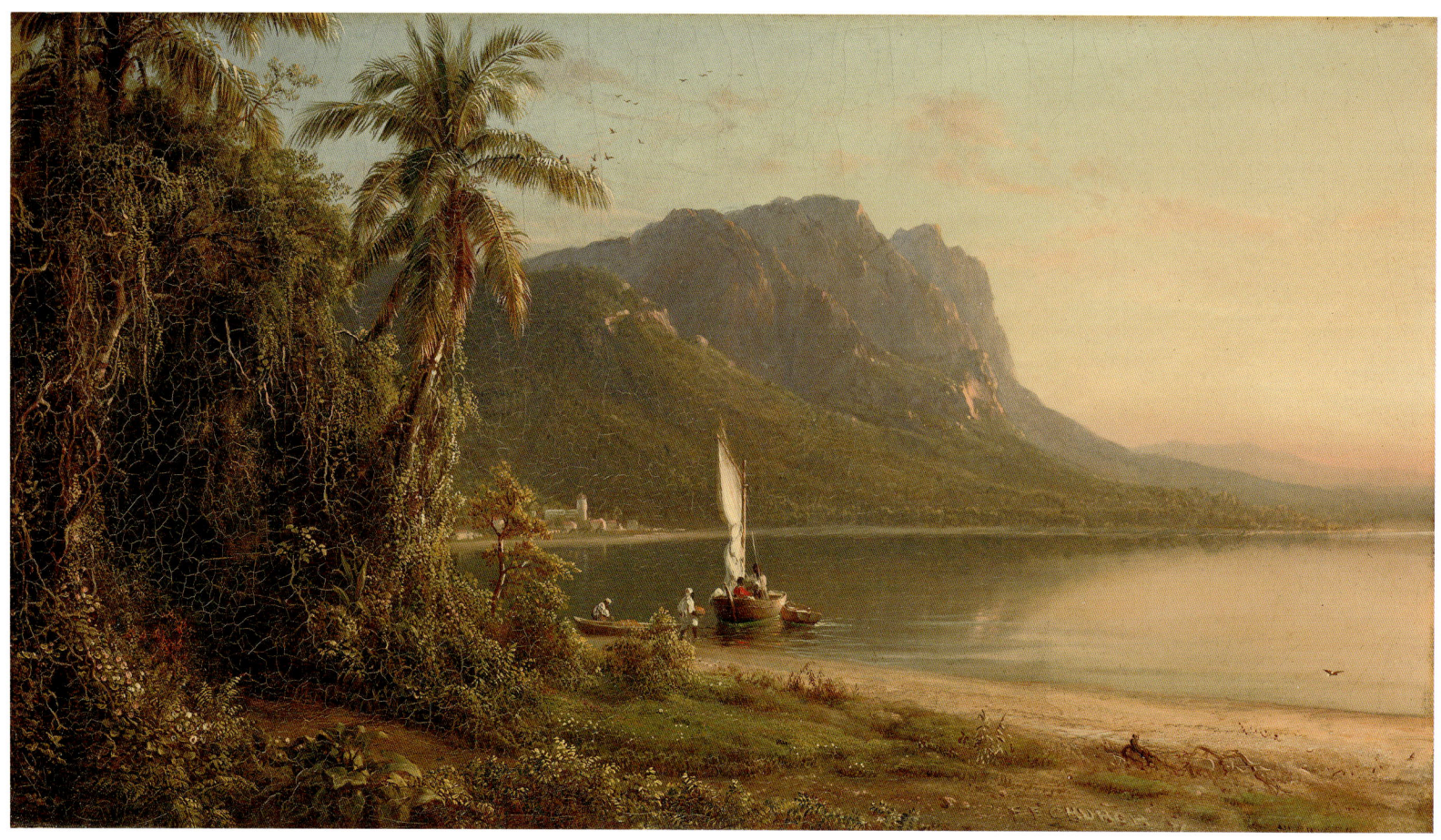

Fig. 29. Frederic Edwin Church, *Jamaica*, 1871,
oil on canvas, 14¼ × 24¼ in., Wadsworth
Atheneum Museum of Art, Hartford, Conn.,
Gift of E. Hart Fenn in memory of his mother,
Mrs. Frances Talcott Fenn, 1910.17

His beloved younger sister Charlotte had died in January 1867, and the artist conceived *The After Glow,* completed in November 1867, as a memorial to her memory. His parents purchased the work for their home in Hartford (Church would later reacquire it for Olana).[33] Eight years after he returned from Jamaica, Church painted a final oil, *Jamaica,* 1871 (fig. 29), for the Hartford-area collector E. Hart Fenn. This small-scale work of the island's coastline made use of several oil studies executed during the summer of 1865.[34]

Church and his family lived with a number of the drawings, oil studies, and paintings that resulted from his trip to Jamaica. The artist used his home, Olana, as a showplace for many of his oil studies, as well as his paintings, carefully framing and hanging these works throughout the house.[35] For example, Church hung *Sunset, Jamaica* and *The After Glow* in the East Parlor and Sitting Room of Olana, where they remain today (fig. 30).

Interestingly, his other two major Jamaican canvases came to reside in his hometown of Hartford. *The Vale of St. Thomas, Jamaica,* the highlight of Elizabeth Colt's picture gallery, not only was available to nearby members of the Church family but also attracted many famous visitors in the postwar period, including Samuel Clemens and General Philip Henry Sheridan, a Civil War hero, who toured the Colt gallery on a visit to Hartford in 1873.[36] Today, the painting has pride of place in the Wadsworth Atheneum in Hartford. It is complemented by *Jamaica,* 1871, donated to the museum by Fenn in 1910.

Church's retreat to Jamaica in search of spiritual renewal resulted in an impressive body of work that held deep personal meaning for the artist. It is significant that a number of his oil paintings of Jamaica were placed in his hometown in the collections of family members and close friends, and that he framed and hung many others at Olana, for they surrounded him and his family with the regenerative spirit fostered by these tropical landscapes and served as a reminder of the struggles that the nation and his family had faced during this period.

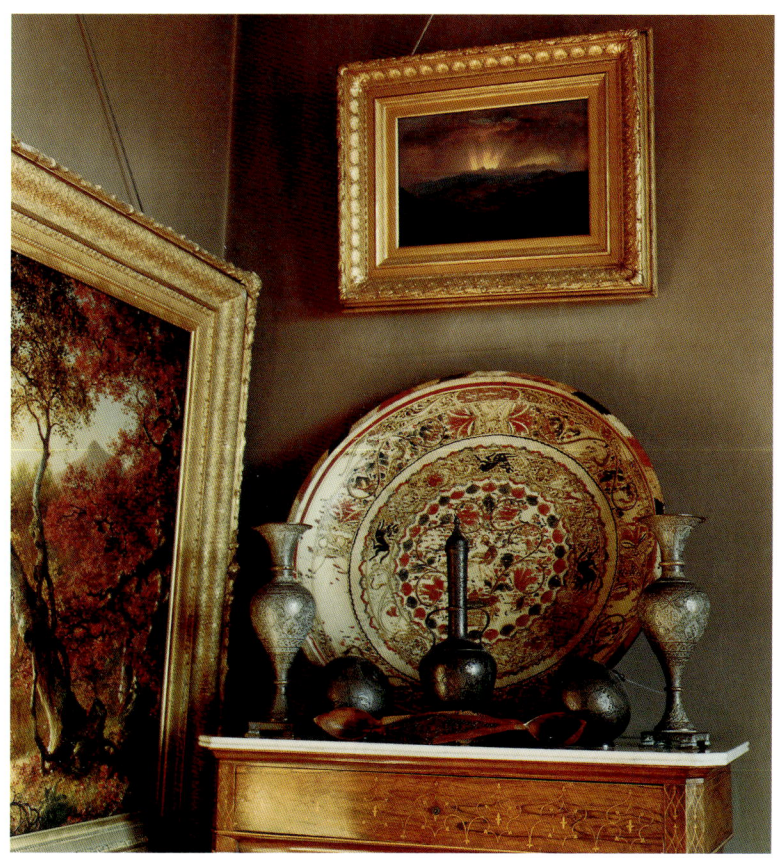

Fig. 30. Nicholas Whitman, *Frederic Edwin Church's "Sunset, Jamaica" on View in the East Parlor at Olana,* photograph, 2001, nwphoto.com

NOTES

1. For a discussion of Church's South American landscapes and the influence of the writings of the German naturalist Alexander von Humboldt on these tropical paintings, see Franklin Kelly, in Kelly et al., *Frederic Edwin Church* (Washington, D.C.: Smithsonian Institution Press with the National Gallery of Art, 1989), pp. 46–47.

2. Henry T. Tuckerman, *Book of the Artists: American Artist Life, Comprising Biographical and Critical Sketches of American Artists . . .* (New York: G. P. Putnam & Son, 1867), p. 386. For the most complete biography of Horace Wolcott Robbins, see Elizabeth McClintock, "Horace Wolcott Robbins" (master's thesis, Trinity College, Hartford, 1990).

3. Franklin Kelly argued that *Twilight in the Wilderness*, 1860, painted as the nation was on the eve of war, "may be seen as reflecting Church's uneasiness about the future of the country," in Kelly et al., *Frederic Edwin Church*, p. 59. David C. Huntington linked *Cotopaxi*, 1862 (The Detroit Institute of Arts), to the impending conflict, describing the painting as "a parable of the Civil War addressed to Union eyes," in Huntington, "Church and Luminism: Light for America's Elect," in *American Light: The Luminist Movement, 1850–1875*, ed. John Wilmerding (Washington, D.C.: National Gallery of Art, 1980), pp. 156–60, 179–80. Also see Katherine Manthorne, *Creation and Renewal: Views of Cotopaxi by Frederic Edwin Church* (Washington, D.C.: National Museum of American Art, 1985). More recently, Joni L. Kinsey has suggested that Church's grand landscape works from this period can be viewed as multipanel historical landscapes, in the tradition of his teacher Thomas Cole, in particular, Cole's multipanel *Voyage of Life* and *Course of Empire* series. See Kinsey, "History in Natural Sequence: The Civil War Polyptych of Frederic Edwin Church," in *Redefining American History Painting*, ed. Patricia M. Burnham and Lucretia Hoover Giese (London: Cambridge University Press, 1995), pp. 158–73.

4. Frederic Church, quoted in John K. Howat, *Frederic Church* (New Haven: Yale University Press, 2005), p. 107.

5. "The rainy season has fairly set in." Horace Wolcott Robbins to his mother, Mary Eldridge Hyde Robbins, May 18, 1865, from the collection of the late Mary Rintoul, transcript in the Olana Research Collection.

6. Ibid.

7. Lizabeth Paravisini-Gebert, "'American' Landscapes and Erasures: Frederic Church's *The Vale of St. Thomas* and the Recovery of History in Landscape Painting," MS, pp. 1–36. My thanks to Dr. Paravisini-Gebert for sharing her research with me.

8. Theodore E. Stebbins Jr., *Close Observations: Selected Oil Sketches by Frederic E. Church* (Washington, D.C.: Smithsonian Institution Press, 1978), pp. 35–38.

9. Tuckerman, *Book of the Artists*, p. 386.

10. Eleanor Jones Harvey, *The Painted Sketch: American Impressions from Nature, 1830–1880* (New York: Harry N. Abrams in association with the Dallas Museum of Art, 1998), p. 178.

11. When Horace Wolcott Robbins traveled to Jamaica with the Churches, he was accompanied by his very close friend "Sarah," whom he addressed in a letter of August 20, 1862, as "my dear sister Sarah," "My dear friend Sarah," and "my big sister," leaving some confusion as to his relationship to her. However, on June 30, 1865, when Robbins was about to leave Jamaica for Europe, he wrote to his mother asking her to invite Sarah to visit "& be a 'mother' to her in every way you can." Robbins to Sarah Hitchcock and Robbins to Mary Robbins, both from the collection of the late Mary Rintoul, transcripts in the Olana Research Collection. Elizabeth McClintock, "Horace Walcott Robbins," has identified Sarah as Sarah M. Hitchcock.

12. Frederic Church to Theodore Cole, July 28, 1865, OL.1981.863.

13. The volume remains in the historical library at Olana, Shirley Hibberd, *The Fern Garden, How to Make, Keep, and Enjoy it; or, Fern Culture Made Easy* (London: Groombridge and Sons, 1869), OL.1984.107.

14. For information on Samuel and Elizabeth Colt, see Herbert G. Houze and Elizabeth Mankin Kornhauser, eds., with an essay by Carolyn C. Cooper, *Samuel Colt: Arms, Art, and Invention* (New Haven: Yale University Press, 2007). For information on Elizabeth Colt's art collection, see Elizabeth Mankin Kornhauser, "Daniel Wadsworth and Elizabeth Hart Jarvis Colt: Collecting American Landscape Art in the Nineteenth Century," in *New World: Creating an American Art*, ed. Ortrud Westheider and Karsten Müller (Hamburg, Germany: Bucerius Kunst Forum, 2007).

15. *Hartford Times*, April 14, 1864.

16. Jeanie Attie, *Patriotic Toil: Northern Women and the American Civil War* (Ithaca, N.Y.: Cornell University Press, 1998).

17. For a discussion of Church's paintings on the eve of and during the Civil War, see Franklin Kelly, *Frederic Church and the National Landscape* (Washington, D.C.: Smithsonian Institution Press, 1988), pp. 117–29.

18. See Houze and Kornhauser, *Samuel Colt*, p. 82.

19. Robbins to Mary Robbins, May 18, 1865.

20. Frederic Church to Theodore Cole, July 28, 1865, OL.1981.863. See Gerald L. Carr, *Frederic Edwin Church: Catalogue Raisonné of Works of Art at the Olana State Historic Site*, 2 vols. (Cambridge: Cambridge University Press, 1994), vol. 1, p. 295.

21. G. Reynolds, "The Late Insurrection in Jamaica," *Atlantic Monthly* 17, no. 102 (April 1866): p. 488.

22. Paravisini-Gebert, "'American' Landscapes and Erasures," p. 24. The trial ended in 1870 without a formal resolution.

23. Kelly, *Frederic Church and the National Landscape*, pp. 123–29.

24. Elizabeth Hart Jarvis Colt to Frederic Church, October 26, 1866, OL.1998.1.144.1.

25. Frederic Church wrote to his patron William Henry Osborn, "I am progressing in the Studio with Mrs. Colt's picture, although I find it harder to work since the Niagara is finished" (a reference to *Niagara Falls, from the American Side*, 1867, National Gallery of Scotland, Edinburgh). Church to Osborn, March 26, 1867, OL.2003.4.A,.B.

26. Frederic Church to Elizabeth Colt, September 7, 1866, Archives, Wadsworth Atheneum Museum of Art, Hartford, quoted and discussed in Elizabeth Mankin Kornhauser, *American Paintings before 1945 in the Wadsworth Atheneum*, 2 vols. (New Haven: Yale University Press with the Wadsworth Atheneum, 1996), vol. 1, pp. 25–26.

27. Frederic Church to Elizabeth Colt, September 13, 1866. My thanks to the descendants of Elizabeth Hart Jarvis Colt for sharing this letter with me.

28. Elizabeth Colt to Frederic Church, October 26, 1866, OL.1998.1.144.1.

29. It was announced in the *Hartford Times*, April 11, 1870, "A large new picture by the artist Church of this city, has just been put on exhibition at Goupil's art gallery. It is 'A Scene in Jamaica,' and is to grace the walls of Mrs. Col. Colt's gallery of paintings." A review appeared in the *New York Evening Post*, September 10, 1870, entitled "A New Tropical Landscape," which discusses Church's painting, listed there as "Jamaica."

30. *New York Evening Mail*, April 5, 1870, announced the exhibition of Church's Jamaican composition "painted some two years since, but lately retouched."

31. "A New Tropical Landscape," *New York Evening Post*, September 10, 1870, quoted in Kelly et al., *Frederic Edwin Church*, p. 65.

32. Carr, *Frederic Edwin Church: Catalogue Raisonné*, vol. 1, p. 293.

33. Ibid., vol. 1, pp. 311–12.

34. See Kornhauser, *American Paintings before 1945*, vol. 1, pp. 210–11.

35. Harvey, *The Painted Sketch*, pp. 91–92.

36. Kornhauser, *American Paintings before 1945*, vol. 1, p. 27.

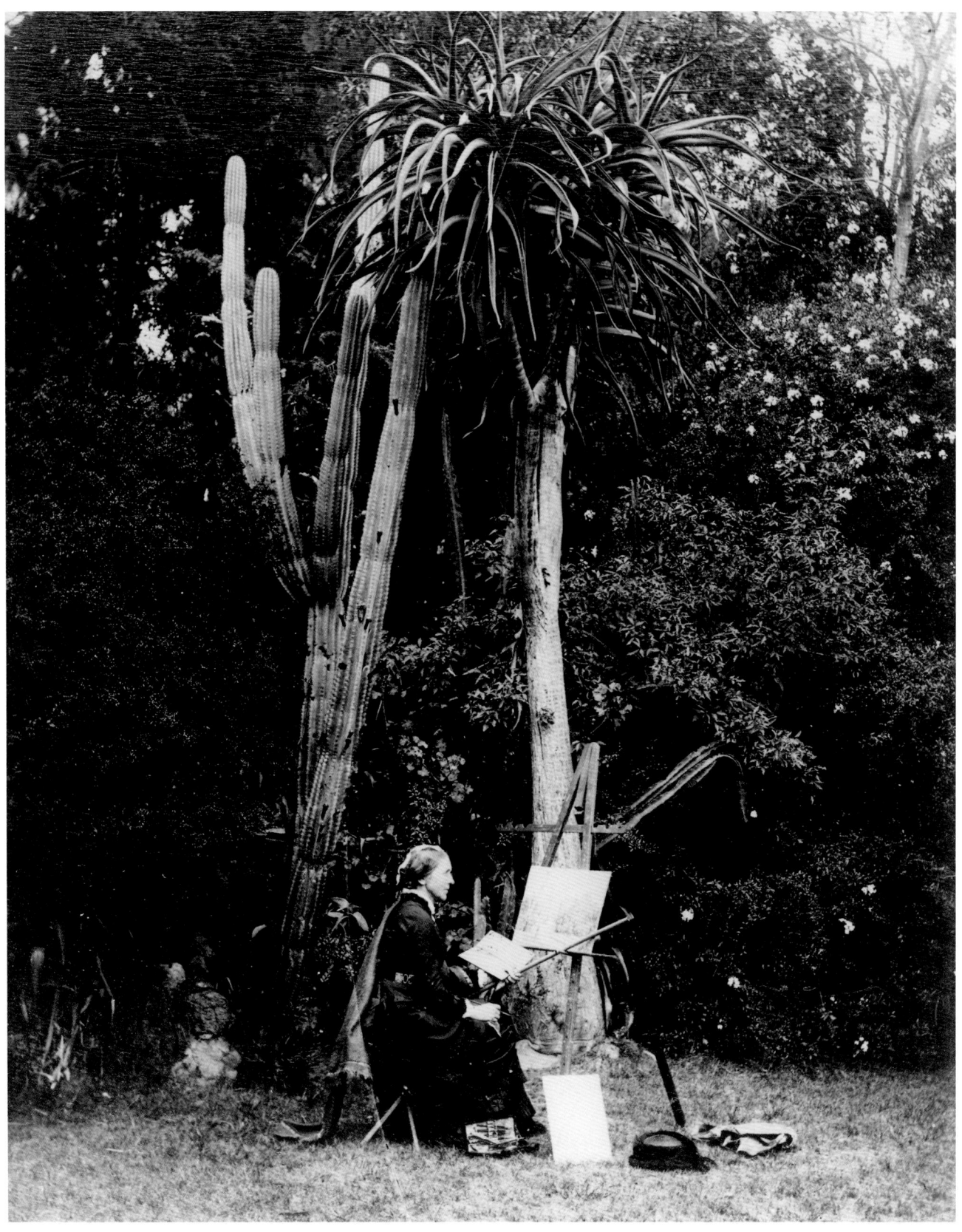

Olana, Salon for Jamaican Journeyers

New York was experiencing a "frightfully hot" spell one summer day in 1881, when Frederic Edwin Church (1826–1900), on business in the city, heard that the British botanical artist Marianne North (1830–1890) was in town (fig. 31).[1] In her words, he "came off at once to see me at nine o'clock, making me promise to go home with him the next day to see his new house, and Mrs. Church, up the Hudson."[2] Although she had previously visited the Churches upstate, in the autumn of 1871, the family then was still nestled in Cosy Cottage (fig. 32). Church's farm on the Hudson River, purchased in 1860, was expanded over the years with numerous land purchases and structures, including a "Persian Castle," and given the name Olana in the late 1870s. In 1871, North was in her fortieth year and grieving the death of her father, whose substantial fortune then allowed her to fulfill her quest to "tour around the world to paint the distinctive wild flowers of each country," as the *New York Times* reported.[3] Church told her about his own far-flung expeditions, often referencing pictures he had produced of each location as he spoke. The sight of these materials inspired her, as she recalled:

> The studio was a detached building, with a picture in progress of Chimborazo, which seemed to me perfection in point of truth and workmanship. He showed me other tropical studies which made me more than ever anxious to go and see these countries.[4]

While she never went to Ecuador to see Chimborazo, she journeyed to the Chilean Andes and the jungles of Brazil as well as more than a dozen other countries, including

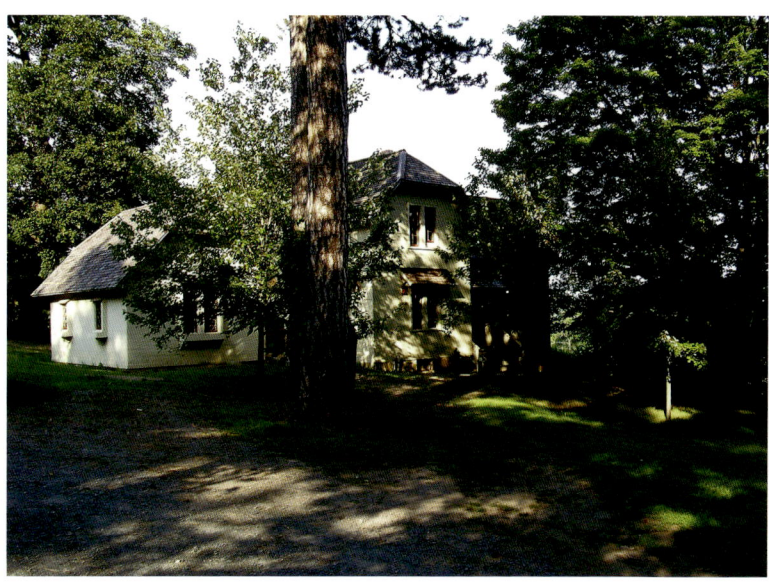

Fig. 32. Carri Manchester, *Cosy Cottage at Olana*, photograph, 2009

Fig. 31. Unknown photographer, *Marianne North Seated at Her Easel, South Africa*, c. 1882–83, albumen print, 25 × 20 in., Royal Botanic Gardens, Kew, Richmond, Surrey, England

Canada, Japan, Singapore, Borneo, Java, Ceylon (where she met photographer Julia Margaret Cameron), India, New Zealand, Australia, Tasmania, South Africa, Portugal, and Italy. Jamaica constituted her first experience of the tropics, and the one location both she and Church had visited. As she described it:

> Little Negro huts nestled among the "bush" everywhere . . . the mango-trees were just then covered with pink and yellow flowers, and the daturas, with their long white bells, bordered every stream. I was in a state of ecstasy, and hardly knew what to paint first.[5]

North was one of a stream of visitors who made the pilgrimage up the Hudson to Olana. Over the years many painters and writers heading for the tropics called on Church to discuss their itineraries and seek advice. Among them were Horace Wolcott Robbins (1842–1904) and the Danish artist Fritz Siegfried Georg Melbye (1826–1869), who accompanied the Churches on their journey to Jamaica in 1865, and Charles de Wolf Brownell (1822–1909), who had made frequent trips to Cuba and Mexico before he, too, went to Jamaica in 1894. Martin Johnson Heade (1819–1904) made three expeditions to equinoctial regions, all linked to his friend Church, who encouraged his interests in that direction. For his maiden voyage, Heade went to Brazil in 1864 to study its magnificent hummingbirds. When he returned from a second Latin American adventure, this one to Nicaragua in 1866, he began sharing his friend's studio in the Tenth Street Studio Building, where, he reported, "I am now snugly ensconced in Mr. Church's den," surrounded by Andean sketches and souvenirs.[6]

"Are you painting a Jamaica picture?"
—Church to Heade, May 26, 1870

At dawn of the new year in 1870, Heade departed for his third and last tropical trip, touring Colombia and Panama before he sailed for Jamaica. He recorded in his sketchbook, "Arrived at Kingston, Jamaica February 24th, 1870," and then filled its pages with mountain views, flowers, and plants.[7] By mid-May he was back in New York. Almost immediately, even in the face of all the details that demanded attention after being away, he headed for Olana. While we do not know exactly what transpired between the two artists, the timing of his call suggests that Heade must have felt the need to report back to his friend without delay. Likely he brought his sketchbook with him, flipping through the pages as they compared notes. And they must have discussed ideas for finished canvases, since Church afterward prompted him with a written query: "Are you painting a Jamaica picture?"[8]

Heade was indeed doing just that. Church could take pride in the *New York Evening Post's* report by early September that Heade was at work on *Mountains of Jamaica* (unlocated),

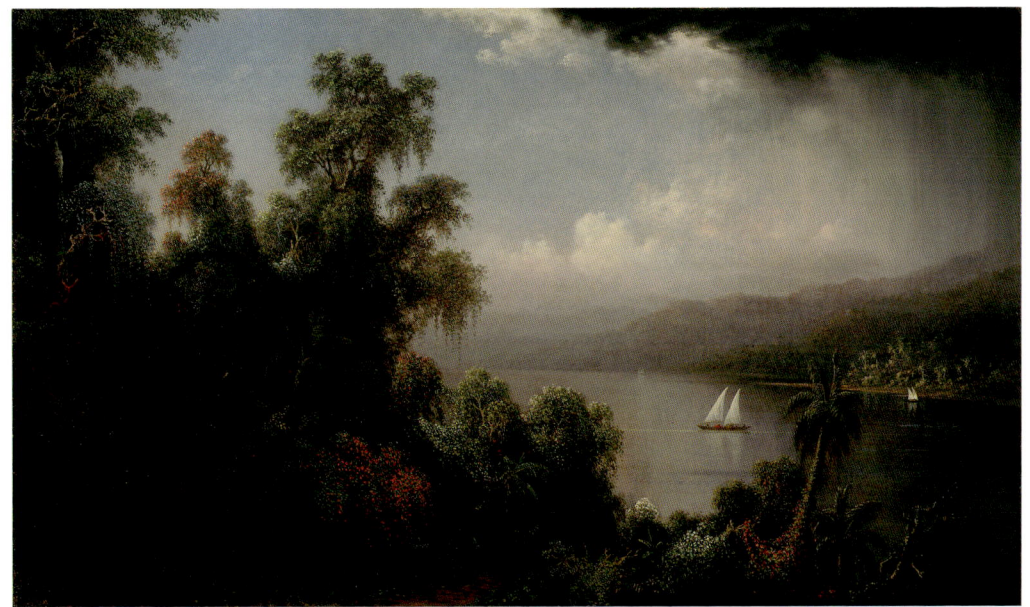

Fig. 33. Martin Johnson Heade, *Coast of Jamaica*, 1874, oil on canvas, 26⅜ × 43⅝ in., Museum of Fine Arts, Boston, Gift of Mrs. Katharine H. Putnam and the John Pickering Lyman Collection, by exchange, in memory of Maxim Karolik, 1981.363, Photograph © 2010 Museum of Fine Arts, Boston

Fig. 34. Martin Johnson Heade, *View from Fern-Tree Walk, Jamaica*, 1887, oil on canvas, 53 × 90 in., Manoogian Collection

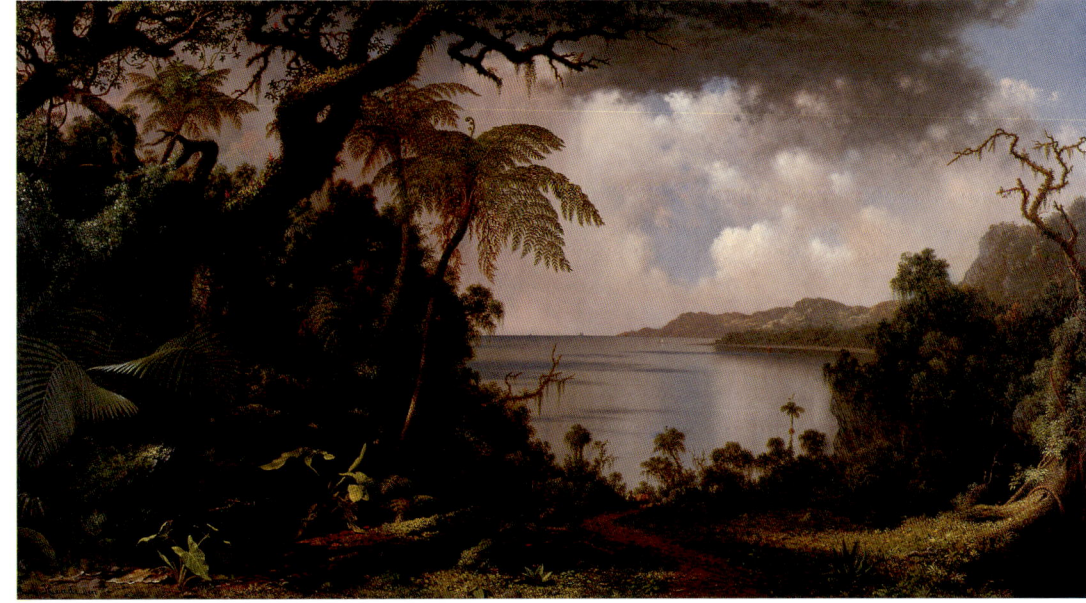

"masterly as an exemplification of poetical feeling and technical skill on the part of the artist."[9] He went on to create several full-scale works, including *Coast of Jamaica* (fig. 33) and *View from Fern-Tree Walk, Jamaica* (fig. 34), both of which contrast the vista of mountains and water with an exuberance of vegetation that frames and almost overpowers the foreground.

Over time, Heade's tropical pictures part company with those of Church, who never fully relinquished topographical specificity, sharing more with North's treatment of Jamaican vegetation. Departing from standard botanical imagery that featured a single plant isolated on the page, both Heade and North conceived images of vegetal chaos simultaneously typical of the appearance of the region and expressive of a state of mind. Consider North's painting *Valley behind the Artist's House at Gordonstown, Jamaica* (fig. 35), where flowers seem to tumble out of the canvas, one overlapping another in its quest for space and light. Her backgrounds provide a glimpse of architecture, a riverbank, or, as here, a mountain as genius loci. But their ultimate

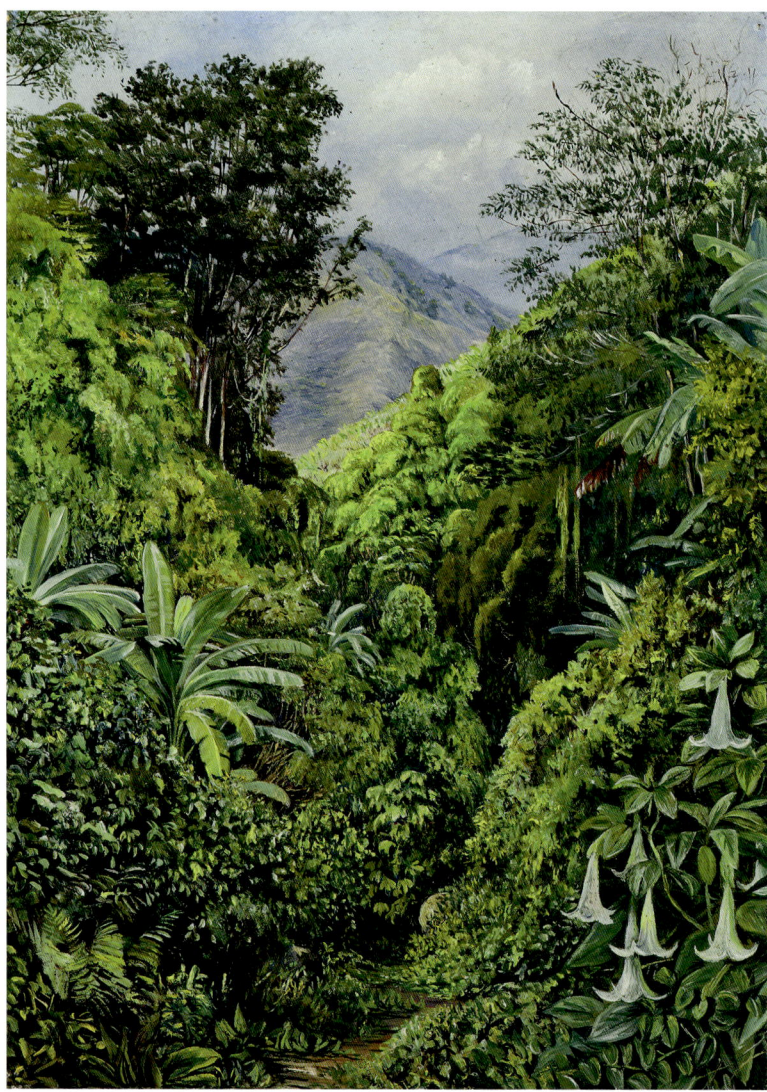

Fig. 35. Marianne North, *Valley behind the Artist's House at Gordonstown, Jamaica*, c. 1871–72, oil on paper, 13½ × 9¾ in., no. 132, Royal Botanic Gardens, Kew, Richmond, Surrey, England

effect is as much psychological as informational. "The plants loom large in the foreground disrupting the viewer's sense of the proportion of the world," as one scholar describes their impact.[10] North noted having seen "in the Bog Walk. . . . a great aristolochia trailing over the trees," and an oil study of this flowering Jamaican vine is in the collection at Olana (fig. 36).[11] Heade, too, discovered the sensuousness of the tropics in Jamaica. After this experience, he loosened his hold on site-specific renderings in favor of evocative syntheses of Brazilian hummingbirds and Jamaican orchids and vines suffused with misty atmospheric effects. Heade made a gift of one of these, *Tropical Orchid*, to Church, who displayed it at Olana (fig. 37).

Church was also friend and mentor to tropical traveler Charles de Wolf Brownell, who shared Church's strong ties to Hartford, Connecticut. Suffering from congestion of the lungs, Brownell abandoned his law career and spent seven consecutive winters in Cuba (1854–61). Using the sugar plantations owned by his relatives the De Wolfs as a base of operations, he explored the island, sketching in oil and charcoal as he went. By 1860 he was convinced of his artistic calling; on November 7 he moved to New York, lunched the next day with Church, and began the life of a Hudson River School painter.

Although marriage, children, and extensive European travel intervened, Brownell always gravitated back to Church as his artistic compass. A token of their friendship was a gift from Brownell to Church of the oil sketch *Royal Palm* (fig. 38). The latter gratefully accepted the work, declaring it "the most charming and truthful little picture. . . . I deem it one of your best works."[12] After displaying it in his New York studio, he moved it to Olana. Brownell also gave Church a number of lithographs of his sketches. In the spring of 1888, Brownell traveled to the Hudson Valley, where he stayed at Olana and made a sketch of the house. On that occasion Church likely urged him to add Jamaica to his tropical sojourns. In any case, in November 1893, he wrote to Brownell:

> I am greatly interested in your plans for visiting
> Jamaica—The scenery magnificent and the vegetation

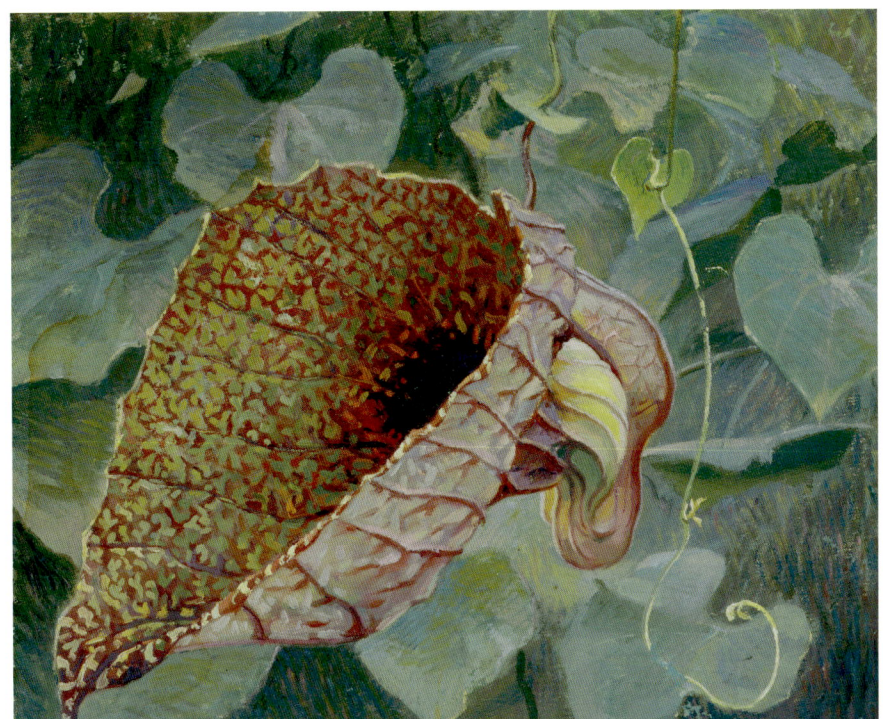

Fig. 36. Attributed to Marianne North, *Study of Pelican Flower, Aristolochia grandiflora*, c. March–April 1872, oil on canvas, 16⅜ × 19½ in., OL.1977.260

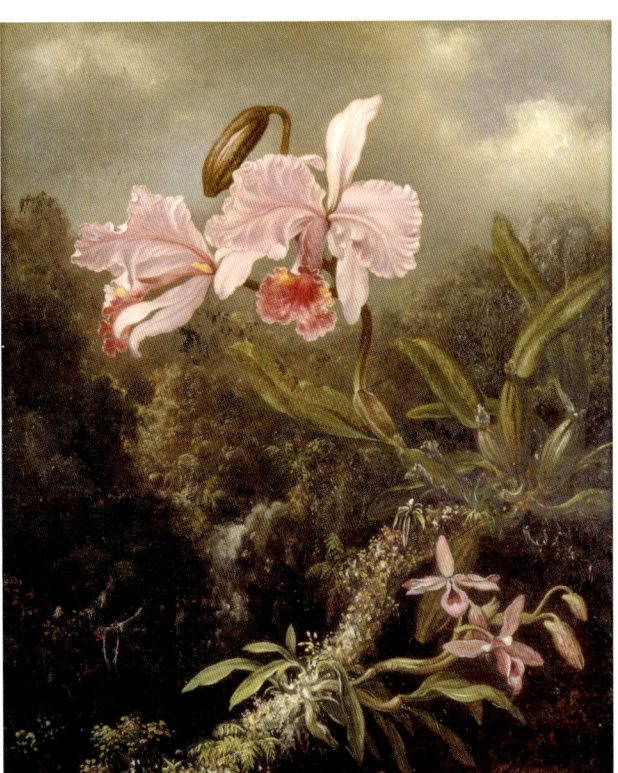

Fig. 37. Martin Johnson Heade, *Tropical Orchid*, c. 1871–74, oil on canvas, 21¼ × 17¼ in., OL.1981.39

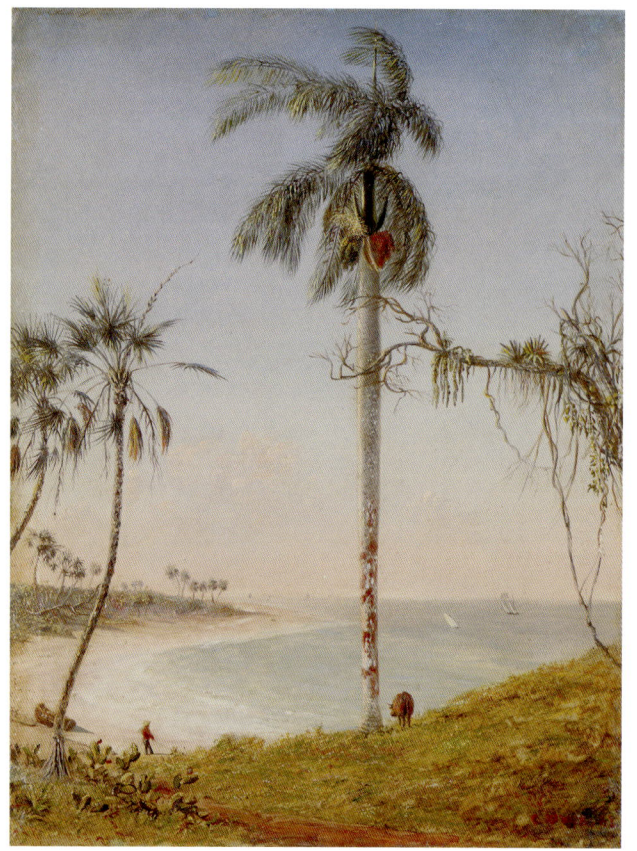

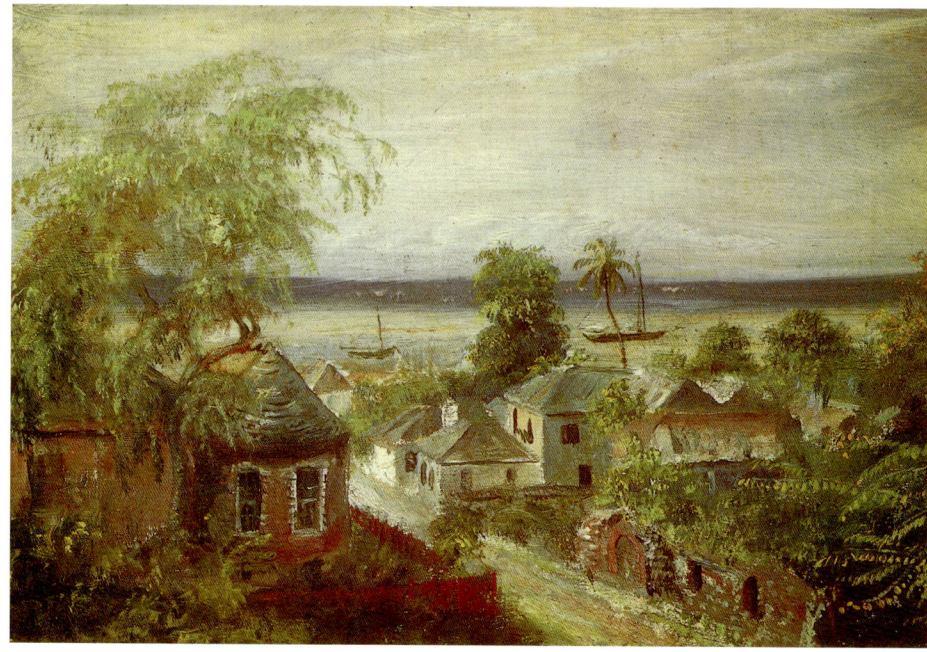

Fig. 38. Charles de Wolf Brownell, *Royal Palm*, 1862, oil on paper mounted on canvas, 14⅜ × 10⅜ in., OL.1981.30

Fig. 39. Charles de Wolf Brownell, *Montego Bay*, 1894, oil on canvas, 7 × 10 in., Private Collection

next to that on the [blank] River—the finest I ever saw— The ferns, especially in the region known as Fern Walk—excelled every place— The carriage roads were always in fine order—[13]

In May 1894 Brownell showered details of his trip on Church, who responded, "Your best descriptions brought back to my memory the impressions I received while exploring its valleys, mountains, and coast." Church's respect for him as "an experienced traveler" who "will find ways to get into the more picturesque recesses" was justified.[14] Brownell produced several fine pictures of Montego Bay showing a view from above the town looking out to the sea, whose freshness and coloristic effects suggest a sketch done on the spot in the Caribbean sun (fig. 39). On June 6, 1895, Church wrote to his protégé, reliving his own experiences through him: "You must have had a most delightful trip since it included some many interesting places that were new to you— . . . Most of the places you mention I am familiar with and so I can appreciate your enthusiasm over scenes which only the artistic eye is capable of enjoying to the full. . . ."[15]

Robbins and Melbye in Jamaica with the Churches

Jamaica provided common ground between guests at Olana and their hostess as well as their host, for Isabel Church had lived with her husband on the island for five months. While he was galloping about on horseback, sketching atmospheric effects and mountain panoramas, Isabel Carnes Church (1836–1899) was occupied with plant collecting. "Jamaica presents the most rich and attractive display of tropical vegetation that I ever saw out of South America . . . ," Church informed Brownell.[16] Whereas the quest in South America had been for palm trees, in Jamaica the botanical holy grail was ferns. "Mrs. Church is insane on the Fern question and is making a large collection," the artist wrote to his friend and patron Joseph B. Austin.[17] He further explained to Theodore Cole, who managed the farm while the Churches were away in Jamaica, that she "is fascinated with the occupation of fern collecting and has already an enormous collection—We have them of all sizes from ½ inch to 8 feet in length." She shared the "great variety of Jamaica ferns" she had pressed for safekeeping (fig. 40) not only with North and Heade but also with Robbins, a member of their original travel party to Jamaica in 1865.[18]

Invited to join the Church entourage, Robbins was undecided whether to go when President Abraham Lincoln's assassination on April 14 gave him "the blues most dreadfully"; he wrote to his mother that "it seems to be best I should go to Jamaica." Along with the Churches, whose two young children had died of diphtheria in late March, Robbins looked to a change of scenery, and to the Edenic tropics, for healing and renewal. Even as he acknowledged to his mother that "this terrible shock—the whole nation has received—has I suppose affected everybody," he still seemed to feel the blow rather more personally than most.[19] Why? Robbins was among a handful of New York–based artists who fought in the Civil War, as a member of the 22nd Regiment of the New York State Militia, which served at Harper's Ferry for three months from May 28 to September 5, 1862. Born in Mobile, Alabama, and educated in Baltimore, Maryland, Robbins settled as an adult in the North, where he had strong family ties. His life thus straddled the Confederacy and the Union—circumstances that may have left him feeling especially conflicted. When his regiment was mustered out in September 1862, he headed back to New York and his studio in the Tenth Street Studio Building, where Church then kept his studio.[20] He likely was nearby when Church learned of the death of his son in March 1865, as he took over the arrangements with J. G. Brown to do a postmortem portrait of the little boy.[21] Only eight days after he lost his son, Church's infant daughter died. Robbins put off his own preparations for the trip because he felt "I ought to be here as long as possible to see Mr. Church & do the last little things that he will find are necessary."[22] The impact of the war and the family tragedy of his friend

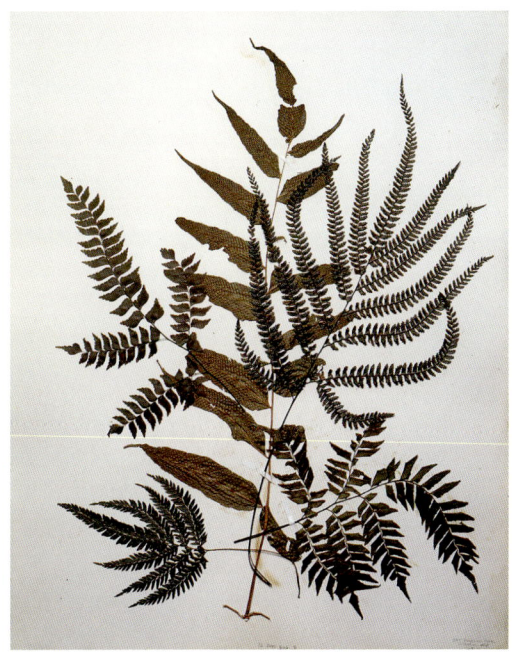

Fig. 40. Isabel Carnes Church, *Pressed Ferns in an Herbarium*, OL.2001.366.3

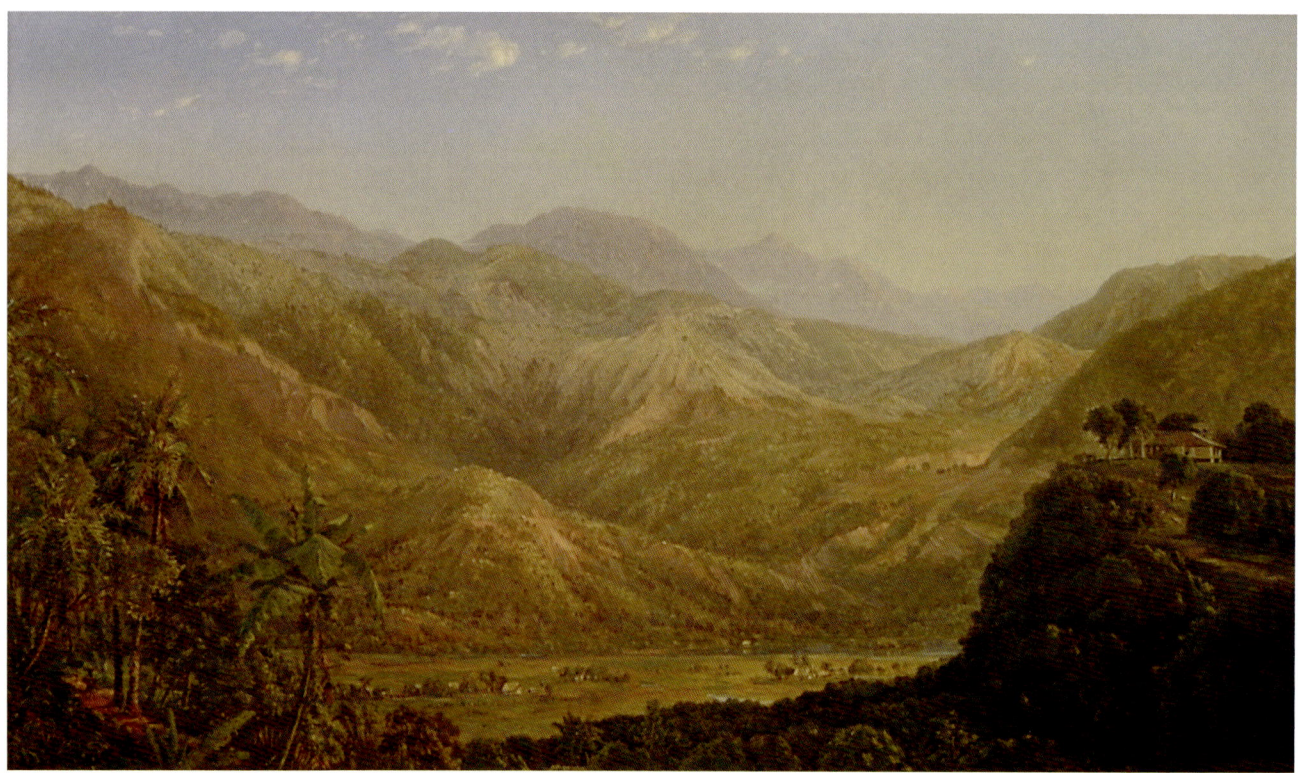

Fig. 41. Horace Wolcott Robbins, *Blue Mountains of Jamaica*, 1876, oil on canvas, 18 × 30 in., Private Collection

contributed to his strained emotions. It must have been a most melancholy party that departed from New York Harbor, headed for Kingston.

Once landed on the island, they submerged their sorrows in a frenzy of sketching, recording the wonders of their new surroundings. Up to this point, Robbins had had only minimal training, and the artistic novice received a crash course in outdoor sketching and painting at Church's side. His letters home describe their jaunts around the island, his profound admiration for Church's skill, and work they were producing (fig. 41). He wrote to his mother, "Every day of my life I am more & more convinced that he is the only great landscape painter we have, he is a giant among pigmies."[23]

When the Jamaican sojourn came to an end, Robbins headed for Europe. On his return to New York, he alternated Jamaican subjects with views from the Alps or the Adirondacks over the following decades. Although few of his Jamaican pictures have been identified, exhibition records of the National Academy of Design, New York, list *A Bamboo Grove in the Island of Jamaica*, 1867, *Passing Shower, Island of Jamaica*, 1874, and *Sunset, Island of Jamaica, W.I.*, 1884, all exhibited in the spring of 1884.[24] The following year, in mid-June, he made an overnight stay at Olana to pay respects to his old friends. We can assume that the conversation turned to reminiscences of their shared 1865 trip, including review of Mr. Church's pictures and a tour of Mrs. Church's fern bed and collection. Afterward, Robbins created a picture based on the subject Church had made famous: *Rainy Season, Island of Jamaica*, a fitting homage to his old traveling companion.[25]

Over three decades, Robbins's relationship with Church evolved from mentor-student into friendship, and he accompanied him on other trips, including one to Mount Katahdin, Maine, in 1877. Church's association with the other artist member of their party, Fritz Melbye, is more difficult to define (fig. 42). Born in Denmark, Melbye was one of three brothers who practiced marine painting, and the most restless among them. While his travels have yet to be fully documented, we know that in 1851 he went to St. Thomas, where he met the future Impressionist painter Camille Pissarro (1830–1903), and together they headed for Venezuela, where they spent more than two years sketching and painting in the vicinity of Caracas before Pissarro left for Paris.[26] By 1860 Melbye arrived in New York, where, presumably having heard of Church's interest in South America, he sought him out. Their meeting could have been facilitated by a mutual acquaintance, Ramon Páez, artist, travel writer, and son of former Venezuelan president José Antonio Páez living in exile in New York. By 1865, in any case, they were sufficiently good friends that Church included Melbye in his travel party to Jamaica, probably counting on his extensive expertise in the Caribbean. Once there he struck out on his own, so his itinerary remained independent of theirs, and he painted sites such as *A Blue Hole, Jamaica* (fig. 43).

Back in New York, Melbye entrusted to Church a large cache of drawings and some oils from the Jamaica trip and others that he and Pissarro had created on their travels, convinced that Church was the most appropriate caretaker of these precious visual documents (fig. 44).[27] Eventually they were integrated into Olana's holdings alongside Church's own studies, his library, works he had acquired from other artists, and his collection of documentary photographs, including *Tropical Foliage, Jamaica* (fig. 45) and *Waterfall, Jamaica* (fig. 46), that would have served as aide-mémoire. Also at Olana are two paintings by Melbye, one of them acquired as a gift, the other possibly in trade, as landscapists often swapped works with one another. The gift, *Entrance to the City of St. Domingo, Columbus "Tower,"* is inscribed on the back with the title and "F.E. Church, Esq. from F.G. Melbye, N.Y. Feby. 1864" (fig. 47).

Two years after the trip to Jamaica, the press reported: "Melbye on a voyage around the world."[28] He was off again, but not before he had contributed to the increasingly international circle of artists and writers gathered in New York who faced south, with their attention focused on the American tropics.

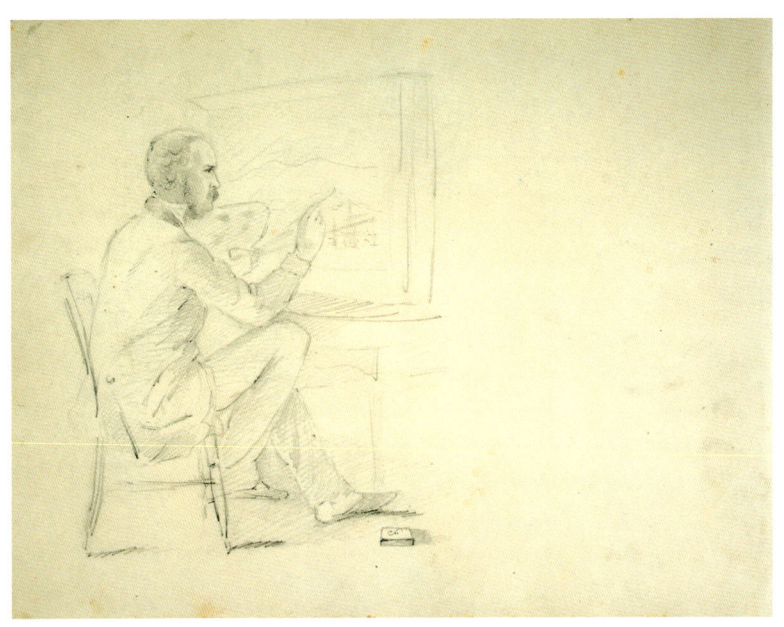

Fig. 42. Camille Pissarro, *Sketch of Fritz Melbye*, 1852, graphite and watercolor on paper, 10½ × 13½ in., OL.1982.304, P-16

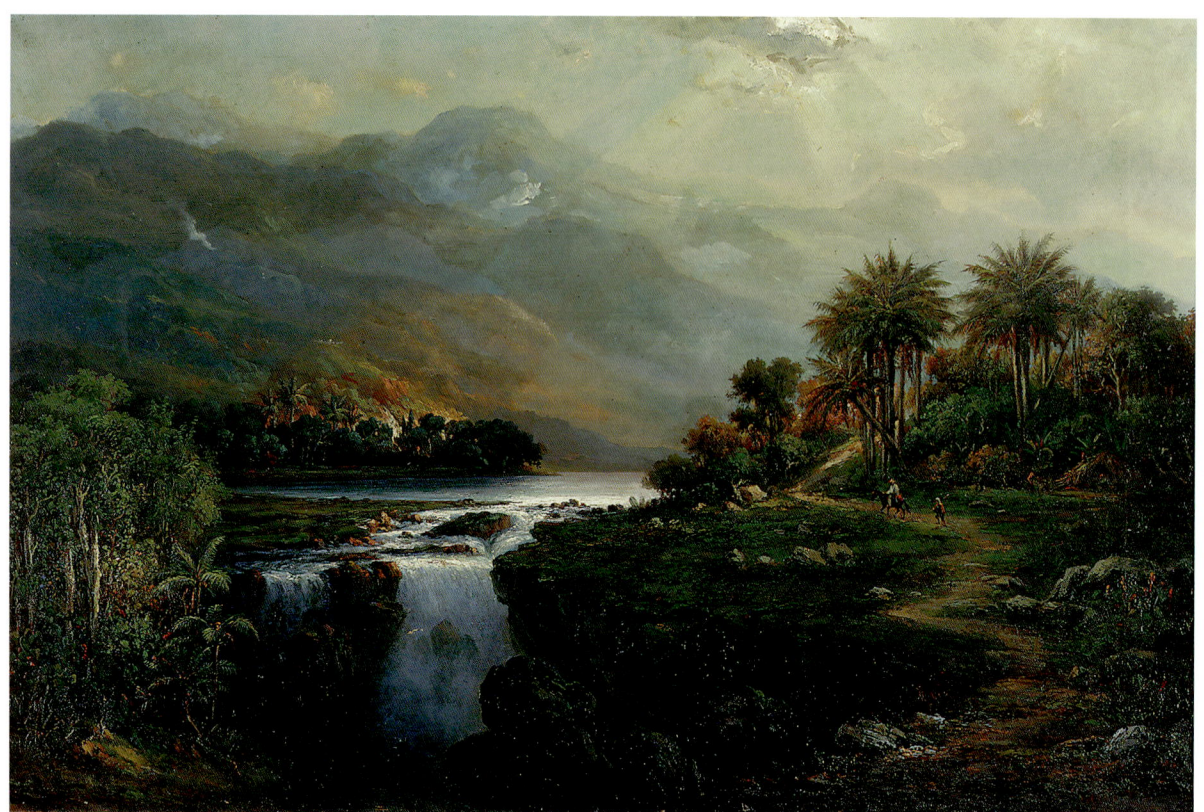

Fig. 43. Fritz Siegfried Georg
Melbye, *A Blue Hole, Jamaica*,
1866, oil on canvas, 30 × 44 in.,
Image Courtesy Christie's,
© Christie's Images Limited
[1999]

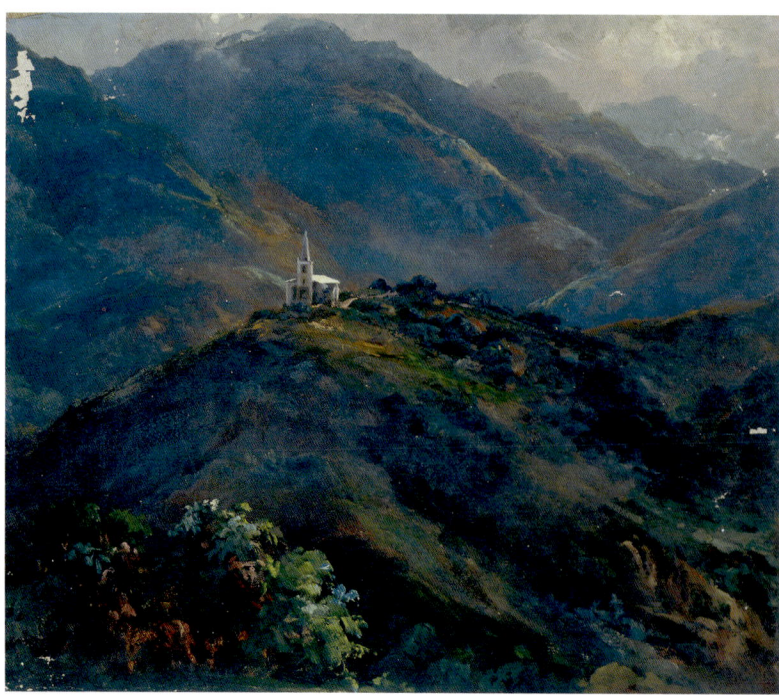

Fig. 44. Fritz Siegfried Georg
Melbye, *Church in the Blue Hills,
Jamaica*, 1865, oil on canvas,
13¼ × 17 in., OL.1982.668

Fig. 45. Unknown photographer, *Tropical Foliage, Jamaica*, c. 1870s, albumen print, 11¼ × 7⅞ in., OL.1982.1264

Fig. 46. Unknown photographer, *Waterfall, Jamaica*, c. 1865–70, albumen print, 11¼ × 7⅞ in., OL.1982.1265

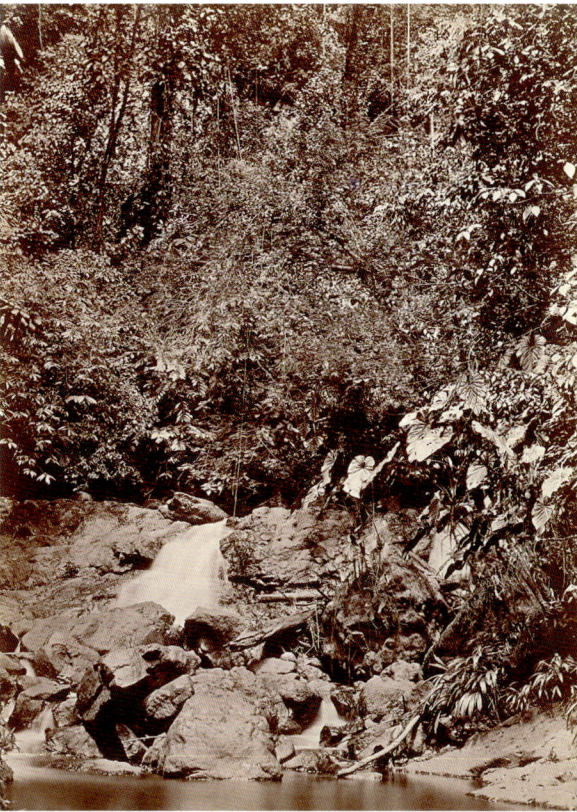 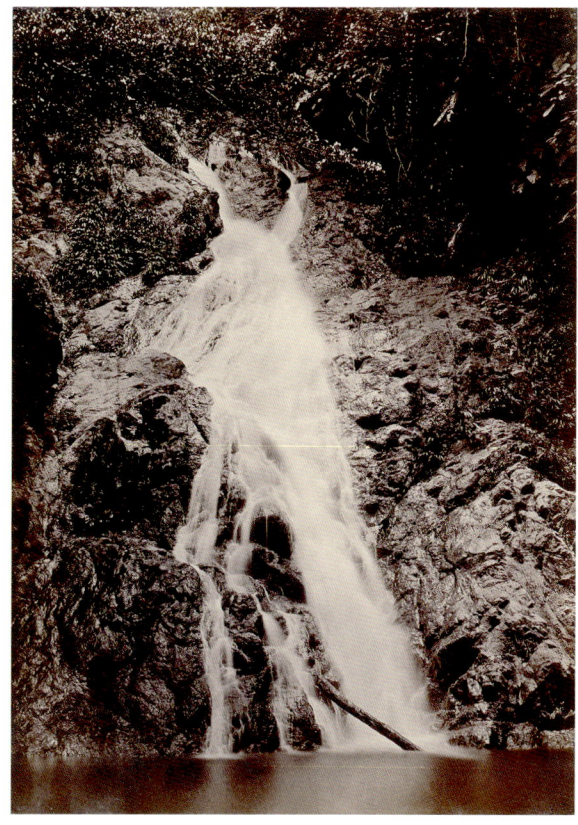

Fig. 47. Fritz Siegfried Georg Melbye, *Entrance to the City of St. Domingo, Columbus "Tower,"* 1864, oil on canvas, 8½ × 14¼ in., OL.1980.1907

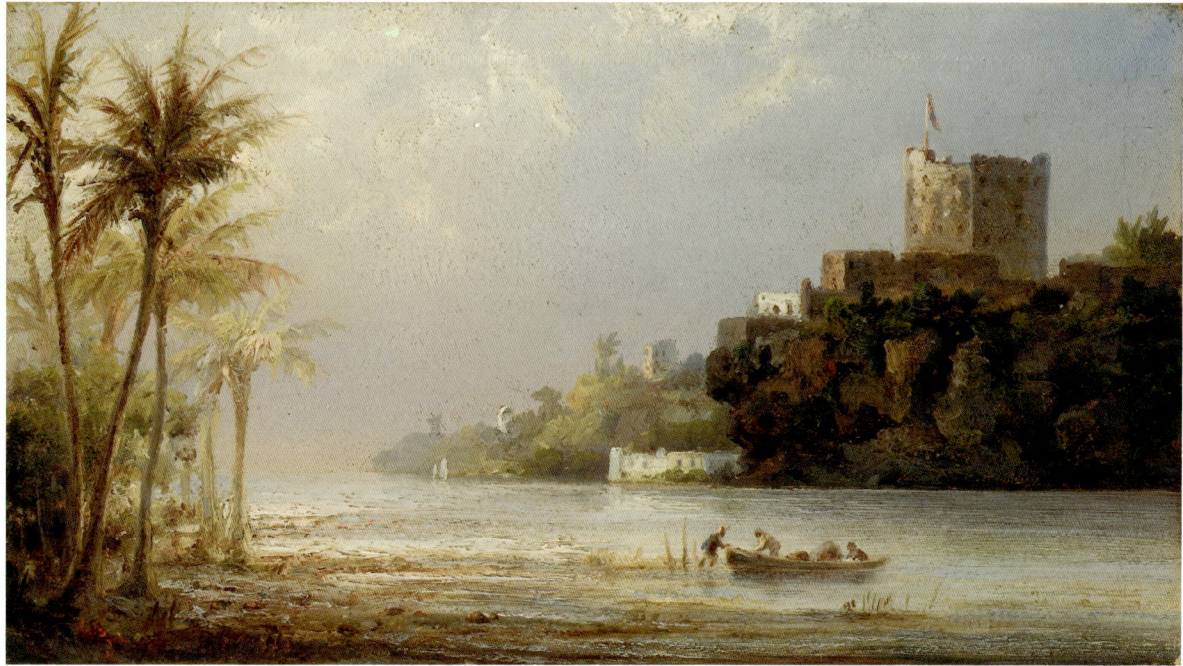

SALON

From North's first visit with Church in 1871 to the second in 1881, she noticed that he "was sadly altered and crippled by rheumatism, and could not use his right hand any more."[29] Unable to paint as he once had, Church rechanneled what was still a considerable store of energy into new initiatives at home. First, as scholars have discussed, Olana itself became an expressive outlet for his later years (fig. 48). He played a significant role in designing both the house and later the studio (fig. 49). And he came to regard the extensive grounds of his farm as his natural canvas, which he composed by digging out a stream-fed bog to make a lake, creating pastures, planting trees to frame the views, and constructing carriage drives (fig. 50). Another dimension of his activities, which has been less acknowledged, is that Church became an elder statesman of tropical travel, dispensing information and advice.

Fig. 48. Nicholas Whitman, *View of the Main House from across the Lake, Olana*, photograph, 2008, nwphoto.com

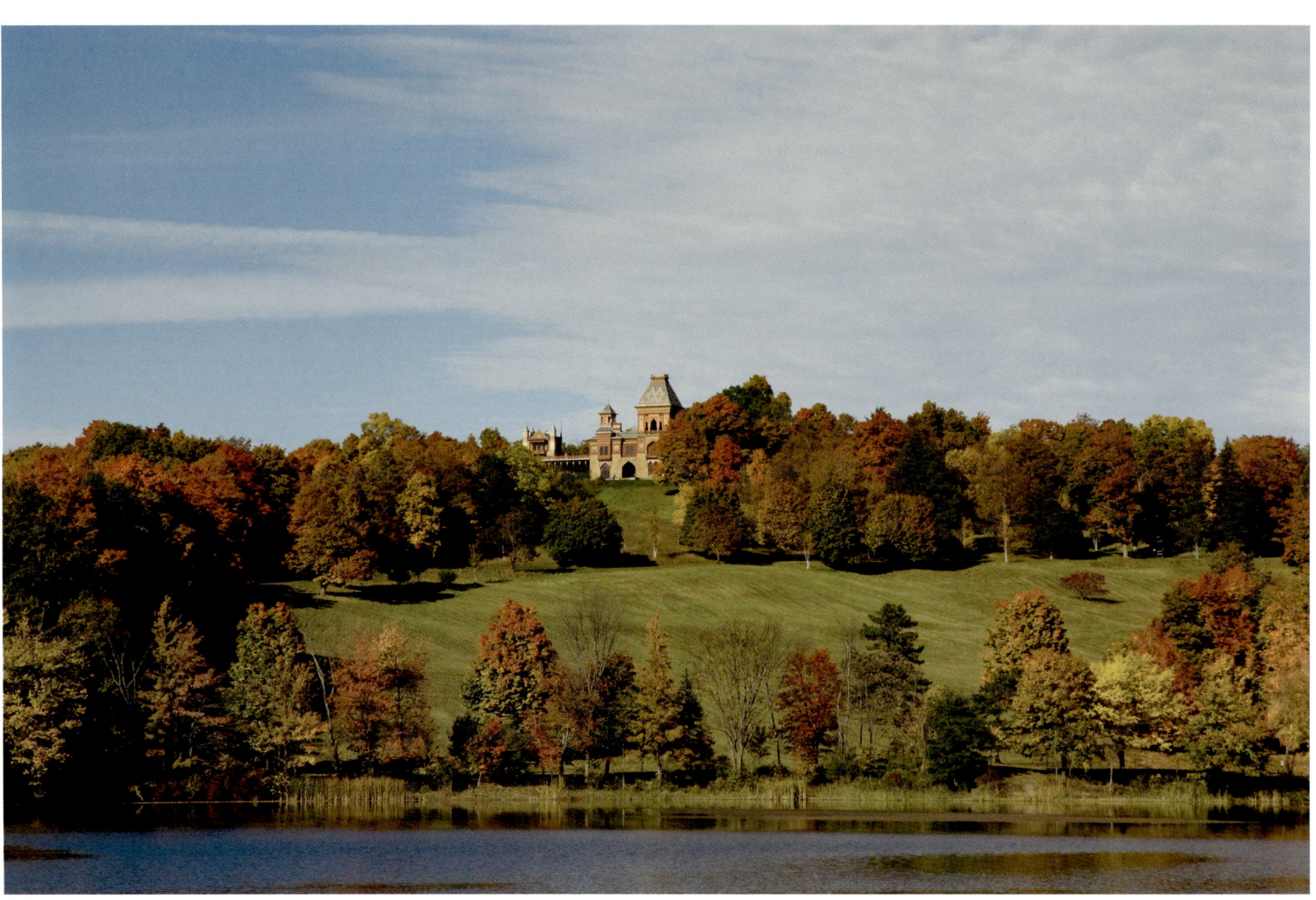

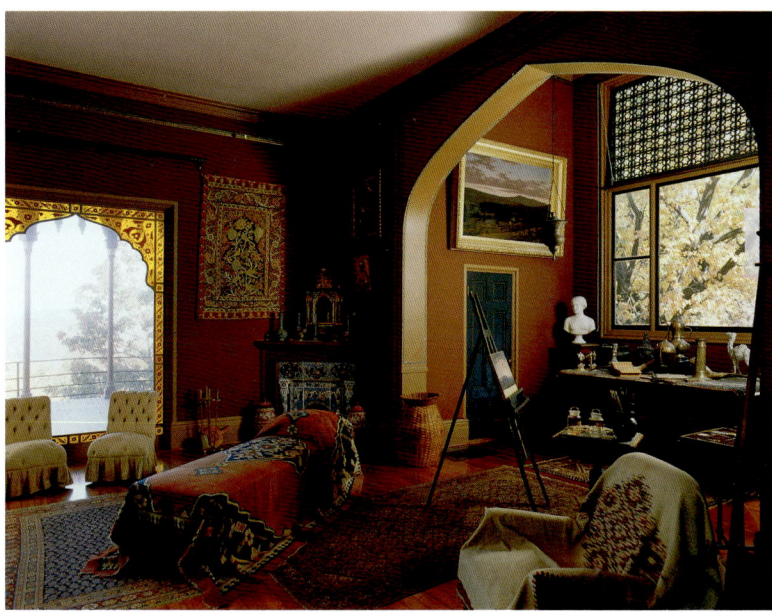

Fig. 49. Kurt Dolnier, *The Studio at Olana*, photograph, 1997, © Kurt Dolnier

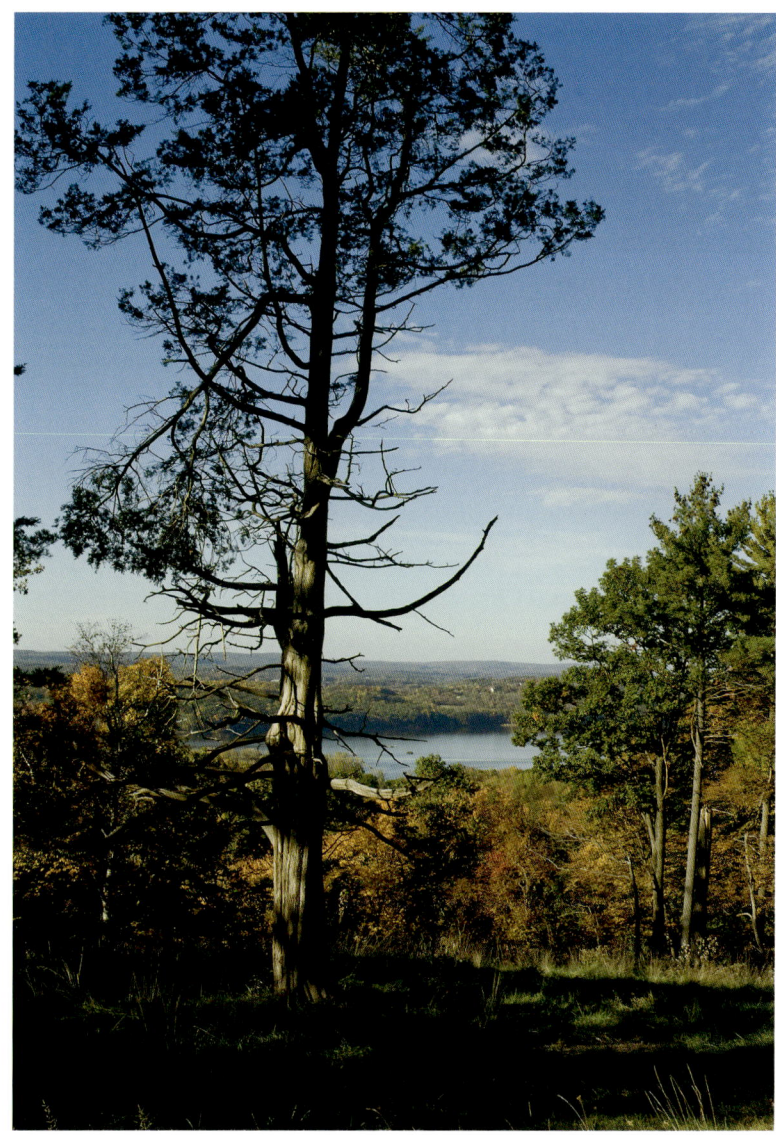

Fig. 50. Nicholas Whitman, *View across the Hudson River from Ridge Road, Olana*, photograph, 2008, nwphoto.com

At the height of his popularity from 1850 to 1865, Church was completely preoccupied with his own expeditions and the artwork that resulted from them, leaving him little time to mentor younger, less seasoned artist travelers. After his return from Jamaica, however, he entered a new phase of his life. He began to function much as the great naturalist-explorers Alexander von Humboldt (1769–1859), in his Berlin apartment, or Charles Darwin (1809–1882), at Down House in the English countryside, who hosted armies of visitors. Some just wanted to shake hands with the great man, but others came to seek counsel on scientific matters, share data, consult the rich holdings of the library (fig. 51), study the photographs (fig. 52), and reminisce about wonders they had seen. Artists brought their pictures to Church, as North recalled: "He looked through all my paintings with real interest; which pleased me, for I still think him the greatest of living landscape painters."[30]

Olana facilitated Church's adoption of this role (fig. 53). There, members of his intellectual, cultural, and artistic circles

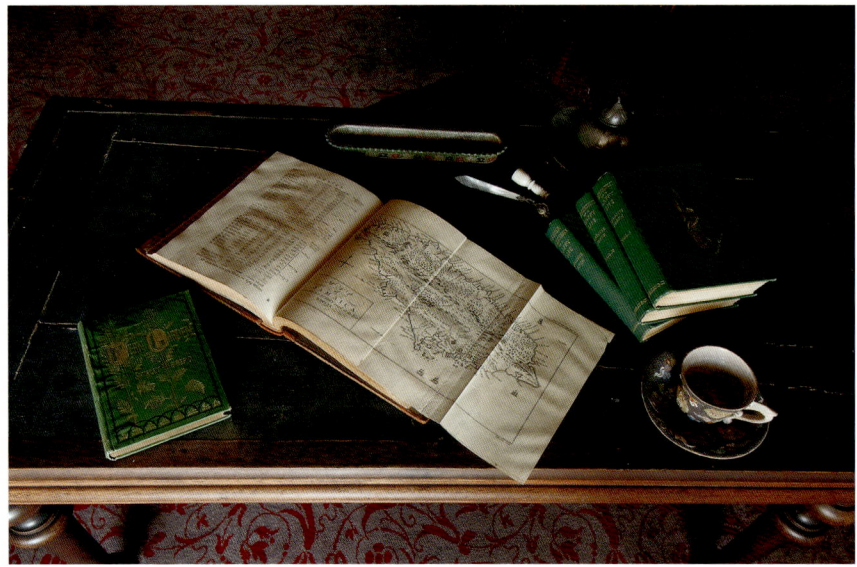

Fig. 51. Nicholas Whitman, *Books from the Historical Library at Olana, including "The Fern Garden" by Shirley Hibberd, on Display in the Court Hall*, photograph, 2009, nwphoto.com

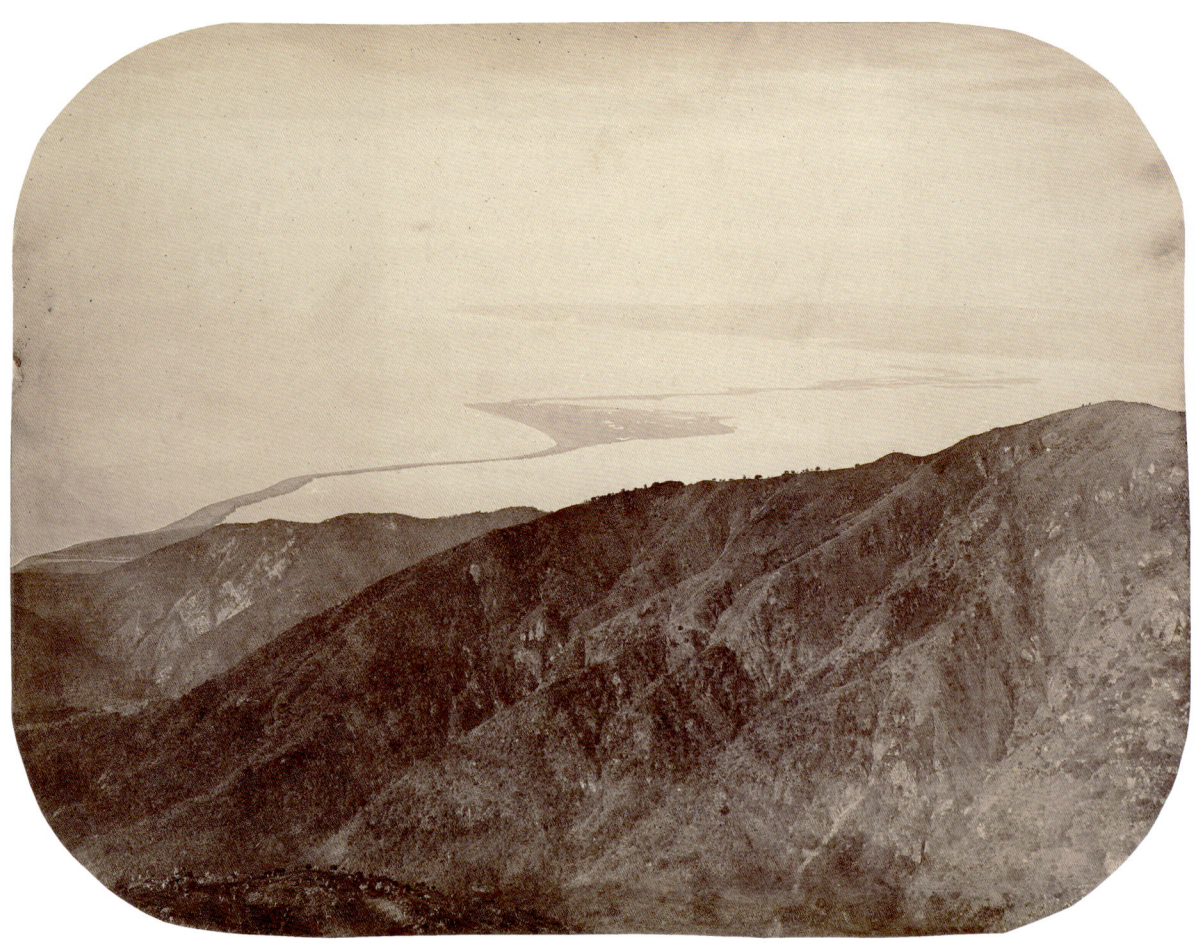

Fig. 52. Unknown photographer, *Shore with Isthmus, Jamaica*, c. 1860s, albumen print, 7⅛ × 9 in., OL.1981.693

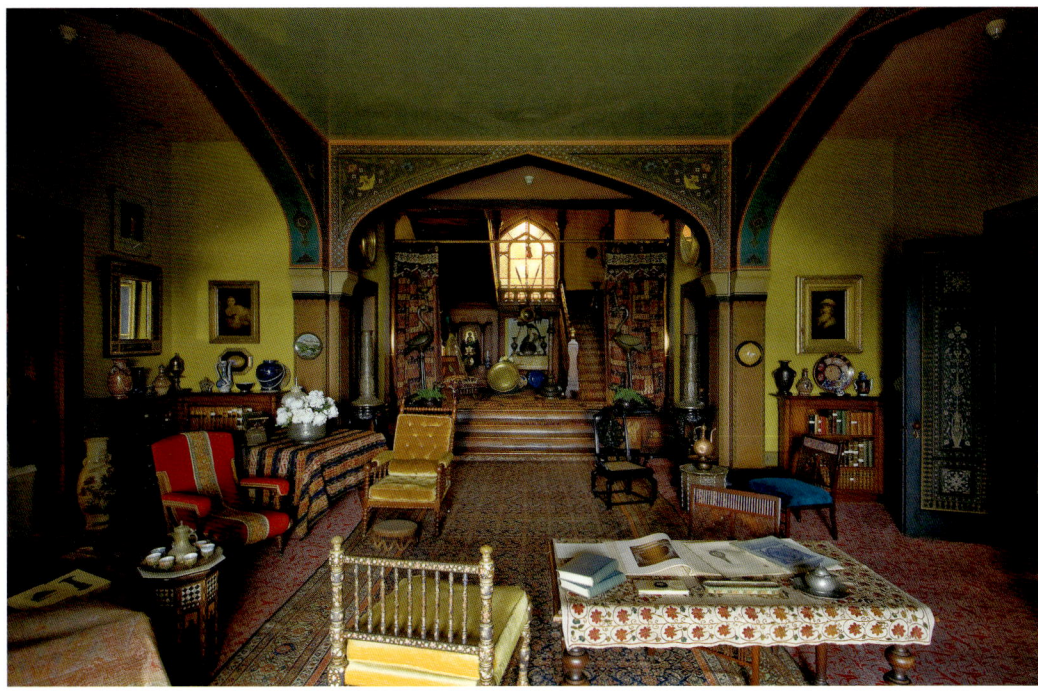

Fig. 53. Nicholas Whitman, *The Court Hall at Olana*, photograph, 2008, nwphoto.com

could gather under its roof to amuse and educate one another and to advance their knowledge through conversation, led by their stimulating hosts. This is the very definition of a salon, commonly associated with seventeenth- and eighteenth-century France, transported to the banks of the Hudson. At their magnificent villa, Mr. and Mrs. Church welcomed visitors into their domestic sphere, including their children, which contrasted greatly with the artist's urban studio on Tenth Street. North described her enjoyment of these pleasant family interactions:

> [Isabel Church] and her husband were quite ideal people, handsome and noble in their ways and manners. They had four children. The eldest, Fred, had a supernaturally wise look, and told long stories to his brothers with the greatest gravity. Sometimes Mr. C. made him spin yarns in the same way to us, interrupting him with questions, and trying to put him out and make him contradict himself; but the boy always had a ready answer and reason for everything.[31]

Church's spontaneous invitation to North raises the issue of gender politics at Olana and the artist's relationship with accomplished women generally. In an age when the majority of men would by today's standards be judged sexist, Church was relatively open to strong women, perhaps because his happy marriage to the handsome and gifted Isabel Carnes made him comfortable in their company. Egyptologist Amelia Edwards, talented

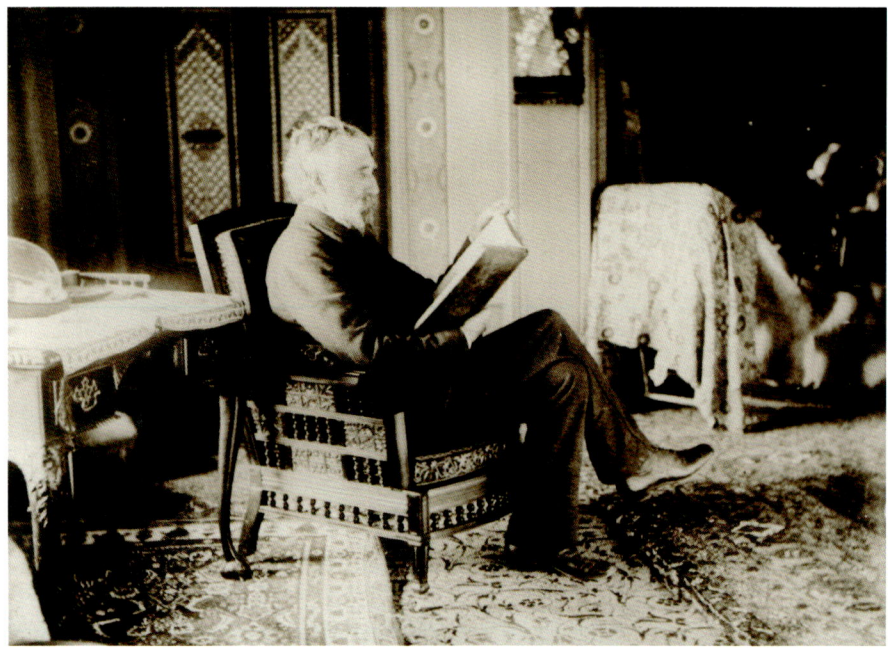

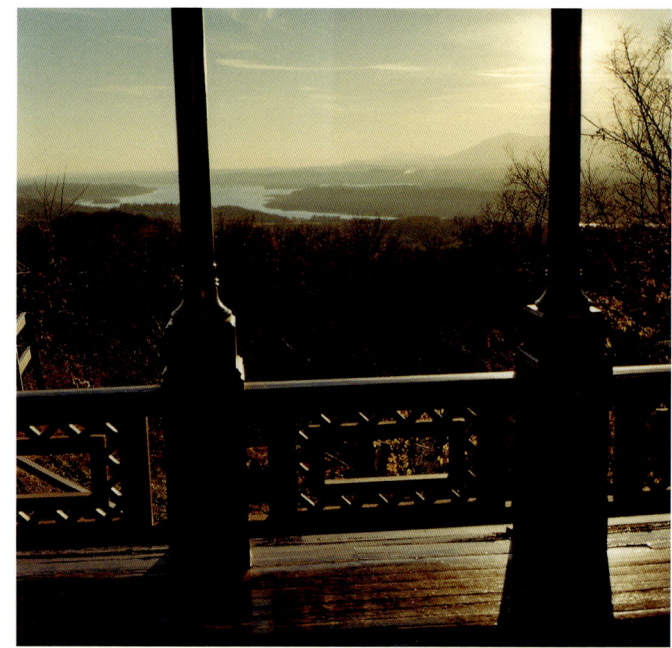

Fig. 54. Robert and Emily de Forest, *Charles Dudley Warner Seated in the Court Hall at Olana,* October 11, 1884, photograph, 6⅞ × 8⅞ in., OL.1986.378.16.A

Fig. 55. Nicholas Whitman, *View from the Piazza at Olana,* photograph, 2001, nwphoto.com

pianist Isabel Fassette (daughter of sculptor Erastus Dow Palmer), as well as travel writer and artist Susan Hale all found a welcome at Olana.[32]

Consider the experiences of author Grace King (1851–1932). She mingled with fellow houseguests Mr. and Mrs. Charles Dudley Warner (fig. 54) and Mr. and Mrs. Samuel Clemens, but when she wearied of society she took refuge in spectacular vistas from the house (fig. 55):

> We were called down for coffee, served on one of the piazzas. Tiring of the talk I wandered around & got into a kind of verandah which commanded another beautiful view—I propped myself on the banister and looked until it disappeared in darkness.

It was Church's art that knitted visitors and scenery together, as King confirmed when she turned around and caught a glimpse of the Jamaican canvas *The After Glow* (fig. 56):

> Turning my head I was caught by a mass of color— It was the lamp in a window burning just in front of one of Church's pictures. A sunset he had painted from nature on the Island of Jamaica. I came through the library after a while to hunt up the others and found Clemens reading some antique book. I showed him the beautiful picture—then found the others.[33]

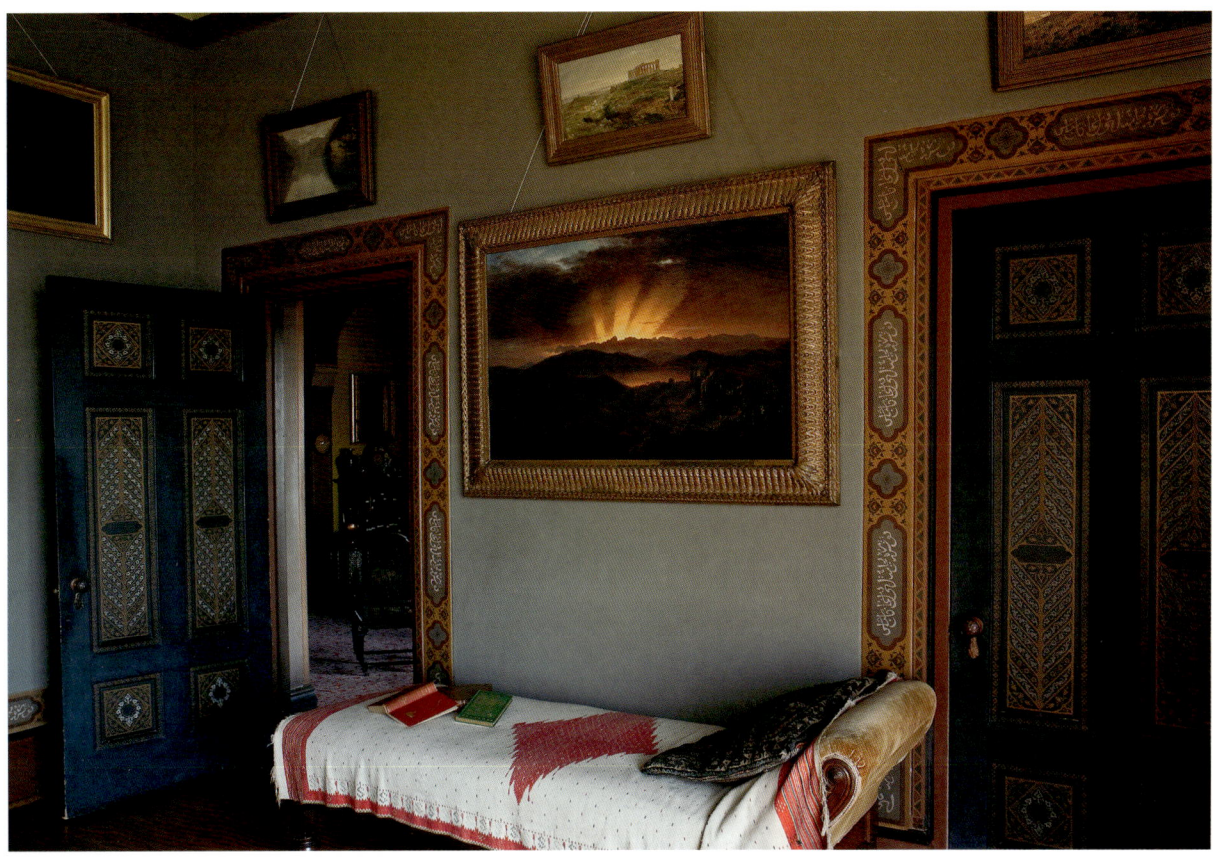

Fig. 56. Nicholas Whitman, *"The After Glow" on View in the Sitting Room at Olana*, photograph, 2009, nwphoto.com

Olana and Global Trade Networks

Church's circle was aware, too, of growing trade networks with the Caribbean, as their fellow *saloniste* Fessenden Nott Otis (1825–1900) made apparent. Church's friend and sometime physician, and an art collector with a special focus on Central America and the Caribbean, Otis, with his eclectic interests and accomplished career, provides another window onto the tropical world. After earning his medical degree, Otis served between 1852 and 1861 as surgeon for the U.S. Mail Steamship and the Pacific Mail Steamship companies, which operated the route between New York and Panama. Otis wrote several travel accounts of the region, including *Tropical Journeyings* (1856) and *Illustrated History of the Panama Railroad; Together with a Traveler's Guide and a Business Man's Handbook for the Panama Railroad and Its Connections* (1861), which instructed readers how to get from New York to the Atlantic coast of Panama, catch the railroad that would take them across the isthmus, and proceed to the coast of California or South America (Church's route). The book proved to be so useful that it saw numerous editions, while Otis went on to become a pioneer in urology. His other passion was art, which found expression in both his authorship of various instructional manuals, such as *Lessons in*

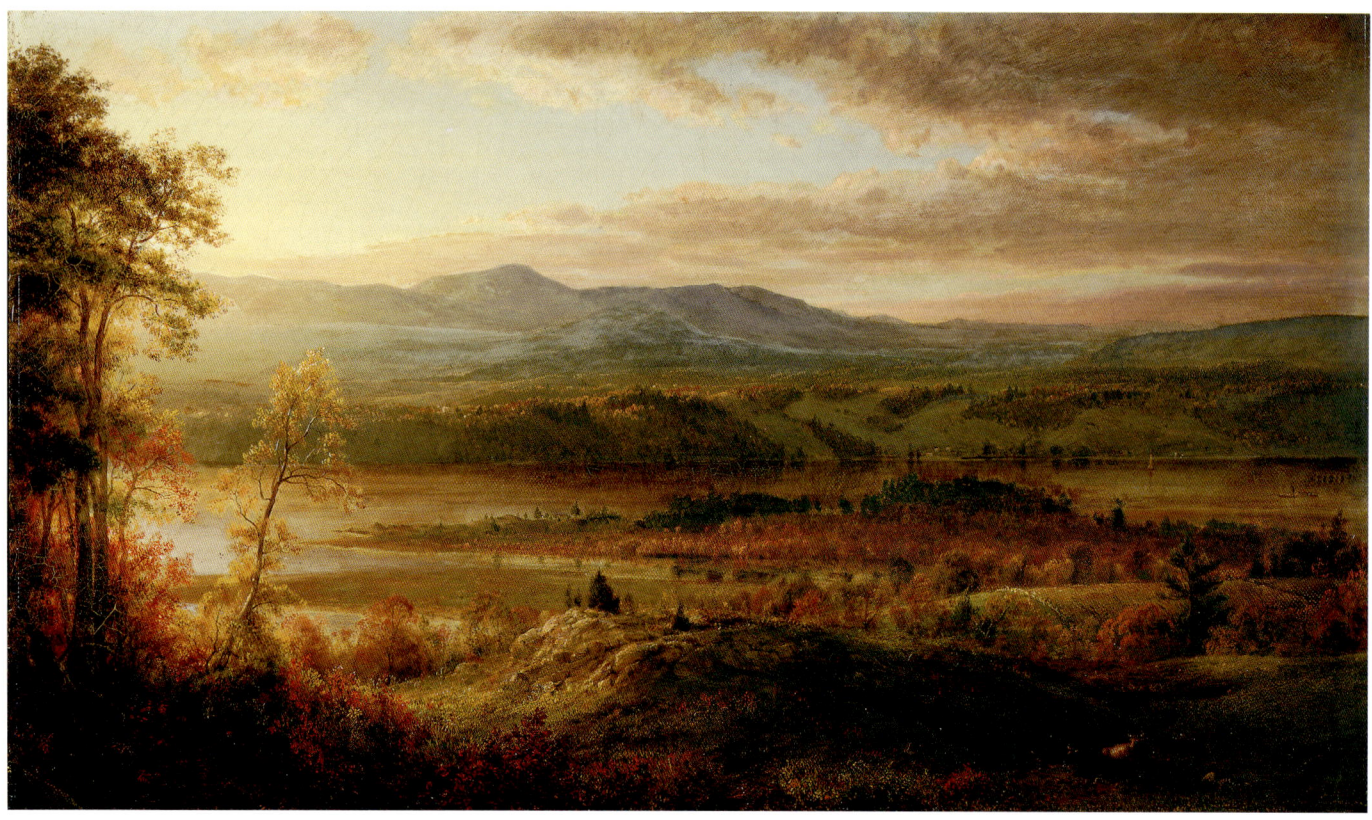

Fig. 57. Frederic Edwin Church, *Catskill Mountains from the Home of the Artist*, 1871, oil on canvas, 22⅛ × 36⅜ in., OL.1981.13

Drawing: Studies of Animals and Landscape (1849–50), and his collecting. Among the paintings he owned could be found *A Tropical View*, 1870, by Robbins; *La Guayra, South America*, 1865, a Venezuelan subject by Melbye; and *The Pacific (from the Ramparts of Panama)*, 1862, by Charles Parsons. Curiously, he does not seem to have procured one of Church's tropical subjects, although he owned his *Catskill Mountains from the Home of the Artist* (fig. 57).[34] Otis's professional service to William H. Aspinwall's steamship line and his authorship of texts promoting it link the landscapes he acquired—pictures of locales made accessible via these routes—to commerce.[35]

The rise of coffee production in Jamaica is a case in point. Aspinwall's steamship line had profited handsomely by transporting gold seekers to California, but once that frenzy died down, it needed other cargo and began to forge links with regional coffee growers. Church was cognizant of the inroads they had made in Jamaica; he noted of one beautiful stretch of scenery, "These are all Coffee Estates." Avoiding any mention of the workers, he praised the plant: "Coffee is the most beautiful crop which can be raised—when in blossom the fields look like snow and the most delicious fragrance fills the air," and he acquired a photograph of land being cleared in preparation for crop planting (fig. 58). He also kept abreast of market issues, reporting to a friend, "This coffee brings the highest price in England."[36] Surveying Heade's *Mountains of Jamaica* in 1870, a reviewer pointed out, "Isolated houses, coffee plantations, and the picturesque tall-growing fern, give character and varied effect to the view from valley to mountain top."[37] His words emphasize that Heade integrated the plantation into his tropical vision of Jamaica. Brownell, whose family owned extensive sugar plantations in Cuba (as did the father of American painter Elihu Vedder), surely interpreted these agricultural complexes as links between the island and the tables of the Western world.

Marianne North was similarly aware of the networks of politics and commerce that connected the places she toured in the United States and England. Her ports of call had been or were still part of the British Empire, where she routinely received assistance from local British authorities in securing housing and transport. Between visits to Church's Hudson Valley residence, she had arranged for the creation of the Marianne North Gallery at the Royal Botanic Gardens at Kew. In the summer of 1879 she offered to donate to Kew Gardens her collected works and a building to house them. The installation of 832 of her paintings represents her personal attempt to embrace the botanical world and to delineate the global reach of empire and enterprise. Kew Gardens published a catalogue describing in detail the paintings that graced the gallery walls. Church, undoubtedly aware of the new gallery, acquired a copy of the volume for his library.[38] In the summer of 1927, when Church's daughter, Downie, went to see the Marianne North Gallery, it triggered fond personal memories of the artist's long-ago visit (fig. 59):

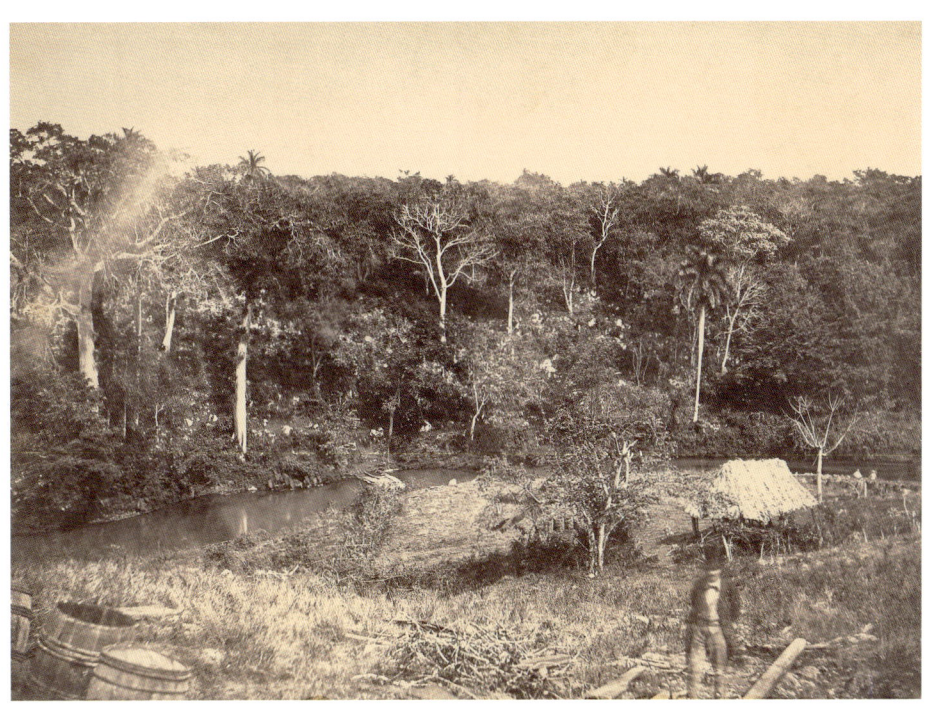

Fig. 58. Unknown photographer, *Clearing in a Jungle*, Jamaica, c. 1855–65, salt print, 12⅜ × 16⅞ in., OL.1982.1256

> Today we went to Kew Gardens—a very marvelous place—gorgeous trees— vistas down greenswards, etc— Saw at last the truly wonderful collection of painting of "Nature" presented to the gardens by Marianne North. She visited at "Olana" when I was a little girl—and showed us some of her lovely painting in Borneo—also two live Kangaroo mice—that she was taking home to the zoo—she went three times around the world and took *her time*—painting hundred[s] of oil paintings of flowers, fruits, birds, insects and scenes—wherever she went—there were also painting of her home and its gardens at Alderly—[39]

So Olana, too, served as a vessel of remembrance. Jamaican journeyers who rendezvoused at Olana stayed overnight and enjoyed several meals together, allowing ample

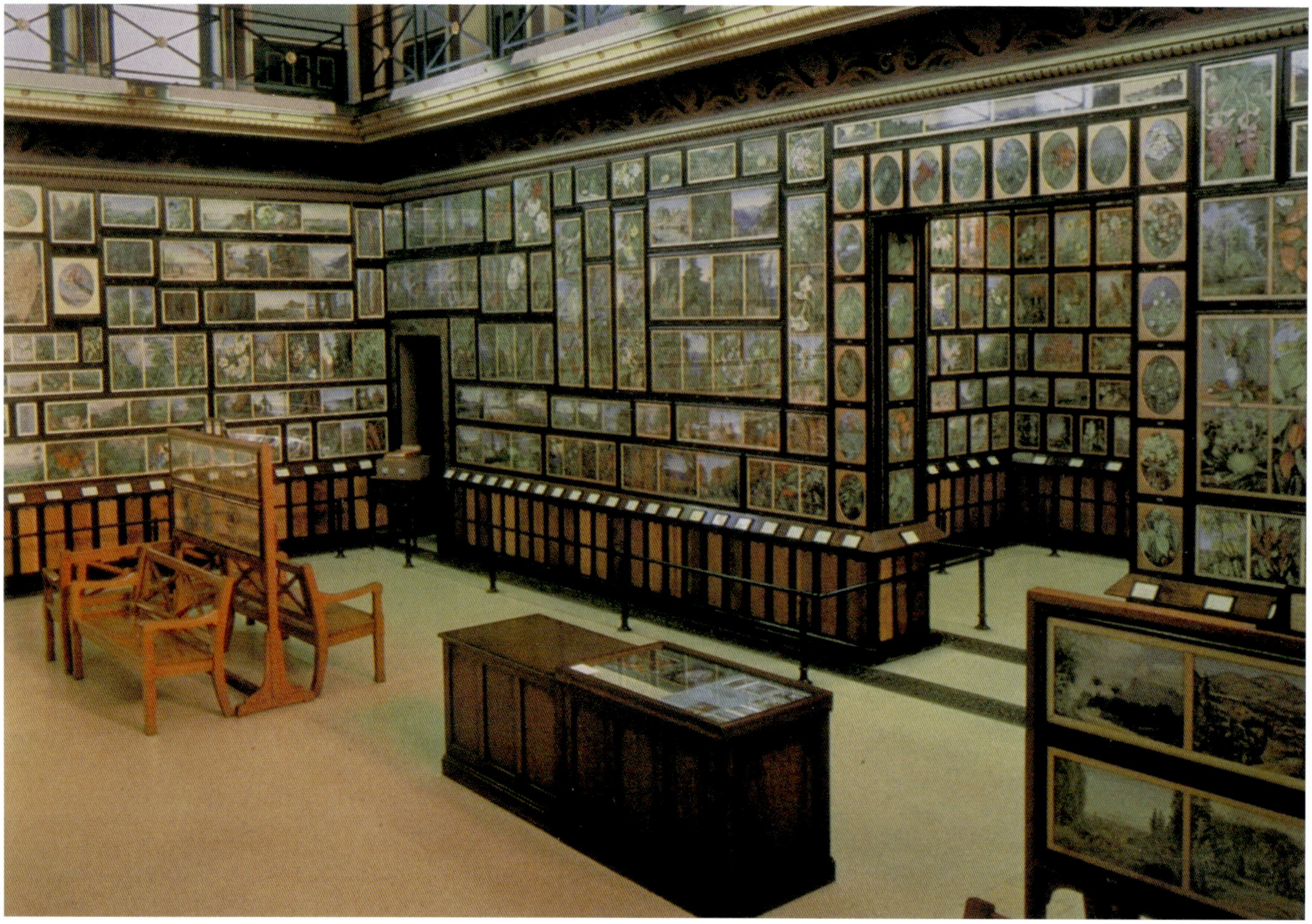

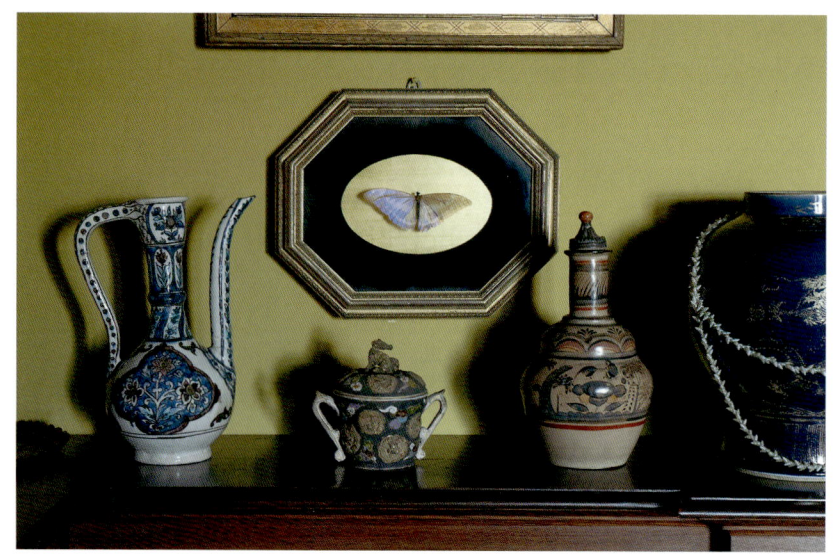

Fig. 59. Andrew McRobb, *The Marianne North Gallery at Kew Gardens, Showing the North and Northwest Walls of the Main Gallery with the Entrance to the Inner Gallery*, photograph, 1998, Royal Botanic Gardens, Kew, Richmond, Surrey, England

Fig. 60. Nicholas Whitman, *Colombian Butterfly and Persian, Mexican, and Chinese Ceramics on Display in the Court Hall, Olana*, photograph, 2009, nwphoto.com

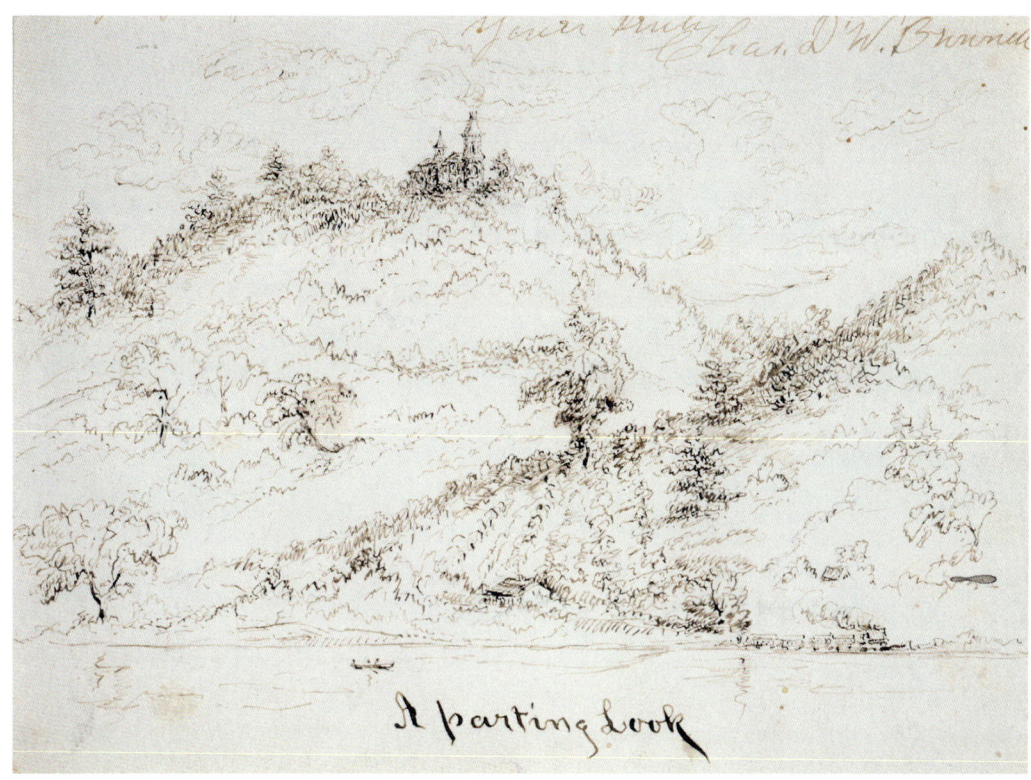

Fig. 61. Charles de Wolf Brownell, *A Parting Look*, 1888, brown ink on paper, 3¾ × 5 in., OL.1982.1137

time for touring the house and grounds and for studying Church's pictures. Guest bedrooms served as minigalleries, as North described: "In my own tiny bedroom were three pictures in oils—one of the Horse-Shoe Falls of Niagara, a study of magnolia flowers, and one of some tropical trees covered with parasites" (fig. 11).[40] The Churches integrated the memorabilia of travel, from decorative arts to tourist souvenirs, into the fabric of their home. Again, North tells us, "[Mrs. Church] had contrived to make the whole collection of curiosities look like the natural parts of a comfortable living house: exquisite Persian rugs, bronzes, carvings, porcelain etc."[41] A gray South American donkey, exotic plants, a "Butterfly from the Emerald mines of Muzo near Bogota New (G)ranada" (fig. 60),[42] and marvelous Mexican birds all contributed to recollections of the look and feel of the tropics that permeated life at Olana. As Charles Brownell waited at the pier for his boat at the conclusion of his stay, he looked back up at the mansion and made a sketch (fig. 61) that resonates with nostalgia for the Salon where Caribbean experiences could be relived in sympathetic company on the banks of the Hudson.

NOTES

1. Downie Church Howe, Frederic's daughter, recalled the visit in her July 3, 1927, diary entry on the occasion of her own visit to Kew Gardens (OL.1987.10). According to former Olana curator Karen Zukowski, the visit that Downie remembered was probably in May or June 1881.

2. Marianne North, *Recollections of a Happy Life, Being the Autobiography of Marianne North*, ed. Mrs. John Addington Symonds, 2 vols. (New York: Macmillan, 1892), vol. 2, pp. 208–9.

3. "Art Notes," *New York Times*, March 6, 1881.

4. North, *Recollections of a Happy Life*, vol. 1, p. 68.

5. Ibid., vol. 1, p. 83.

6. Martin Johnson Heade to John Russell Bartlett, August 10, 1866, John Russell Bartlett Papers, John Crater Brown Library, Brown University, Providence, R.I., quoted in Theodore E. Stebbins Jr., *The Life and Works of Martin Johnson Heade* (New Haven: Yale University Press, 2000), p. 80.

7. Martin Johnson Heade, *The Jamaica Sketchbook*, inscribed cover, verso, Museum of Fine Arts, Boston, Gift of Susan and Richard Nash, 1997.297.

8. Frederic Church to Martin Johnson Heade, May 26, 1870, Martin Johnson Heade Papers, 1853–1904, Archives of American Art, Smithsonian Institution, Washington, D.C.

9. *New York Evening Post*, September 10, 1870, quoted in Stebbins, *The Life and Work of Martin Johnson Heade*, p. 174, cat. no. 190.

10. Antonia Losano, "A Preference for Vegetables: The Travel Writings and Botanical Art of Marianne North," *Women's Studies* 26 (1997): p. 443.

11. North, *Recollections of a Happy Life*, vol. 1, p. 99. This study and a second of a bird-of-paradise in Olana's collection are possibly by Marianne North. These tentative identifications were made by Olana's Curatorial Department.

12. Frederic Church to Charles de Wolf Brownell, August 1, 1862, copy from an unknown source, transcript in the Olana Research Collection.

13. Frederic Church to Brownell, November 6, 1893, copy from an unknown source, transcript in the Olana Research Collection.

14. Frederic Church to Brownell, May 30, 1894, copy from an unknown source, transcript in the Olana Research Collection.

15. Frederic Church to Brownell, June 6, 1895, copy from an unknown source, transcript in the Olana Research Collection.

16. Frederic Church to Brownell, May 30, 1894.

17. Frederic Church to [Joseph B.] Austin, August 14, 1865, OL.1985.63.

18. Frederic Church to Theodore Cole, July 28, 1865, OL.1981.863.

19. Horace Wolcott Robbins to his mother, Mary Eldridge Hyde Robbins, April 16, 1865, from the collection of the late Mary Rintoul, transcript in the Olana Research Collection.

20. Frederick Phisterer, *New York in the War of the Rebellion* (Albany, N.Y.: J. B. Lyon, 1912), provides general background on the regiment; the Web site of Civil War Soldiers and Sailors System—http://www.itd.nps.gov/cwss/—includes a citation to Robbins.

21. Robbins was residing in the Tenth Street Studio building from 1862 to 1868 and from 1882 to 1888.

22. Horace Robbins to Mary Robbins, April 16, 1865.

23. Horace Robbins to Mary Robbins, June 30, 1865, from Jamaica, p. 4, from the collection of the late Mary Rintoul, transcript in the Olana Research Collection.

24. Maria Naylor, ed., *The National Academy of Design Exhibition Record, 1861–1900*, 2 vols. (New York: Kennedy Galleries, 1973), vol. 2, 796–98.

25. The painting (1887, unlocated) is listed in ibid., vol. 2, p. 798, as for sale for $250.

26. See Katherine E. Manthorne, "Caribbean Beginnings: Camille Pissarro," *Latin American Art* 2 (Summer 1990): pp. 30–35.

27. For the most recent assessment, see Richard R. Brettell, *Camille Pissarro in the Caribbean, 1850–1855: Drawings from the Collection at Olana* (St. Thomas, U.S.V.I.: Hebrew Congregation of St. Thomas; New York: New York State Office of Parks, Recreation and Historic Preservation, 1996).

28. "Topics of the Day," *Brooklyn Eagle*, August 28, 1867, p. 2.

29. North, *Recollections of a Happy Life*, vol. 1, p. 208.

30. Ibid.

31. Ibid., vol. 1, pp. 67–68, writing about her 1871 visit.

32. While space for discussion of gender politics at Olana is limited here, it does bear further examination.

33. Grace King to her sister May King McDowell, June 7, 1887, Special Collections, Hill Memorial Library, Louisiana State University Libraries, Baton Rouge, La. During Grace King's stay at Olana, a Mr. Twitchell was also there, and Church's patrons Mr. and Mrs. William H. Osborn dropped in for the day.

34. *Catalogue of the Private Collection of Modern Paintings and Bronzes Belonging to Dr. F. N. Otis of This City* (New York: Ortgies, 1890). Church bought his picture back at the sale held at the "Fifth Avenue Art Galleries, Auction, Dec. 1890."

35. These links between art, trade, and tourism require further investigation. For a biography of Otis, see the entry in James Grant Wilson et al., eds., *Appleton's Cyclopedia of American Biography* (New York: D. Appleton's, 1887–89), available at www.famousamericans.net/fessendennottotis/;

and John Haskell Kemble, "The Panama Route to the Pacific Coast, 1848–1869," *Pacific Historical Review* 7 (March 1938): pp. 1–13.

36. Frederic Church to Theodore Cole, July 28, 1865, OL.1981.863.

37. *New York Evening Post*, September 10, 1870, quoted in Stebbins, *The Life and Work of Martin Johnson Heade*, p. 250.

38. *The Gallery of Marianne North's Paintings of Plants and Their Homes, Royal Garden Kew, Descriptive Catalog Compiled by W. Botting Hemsley, A.L.S.* (London: Spottiswoods, 1882), OL.1986.115.

39. Howe, diary entry of July 3, 1927, OL.1987.10.

40. North, *Recollections of a Happy Life*, vol. 1, p. 68. Her description of the bedroom at Cosy Cottage applies to the "Persian Castle" as well.

41. North, *Recollections of a Happy Life*, vol. 2, p. 209.

42. This is the inscription on the back of the frame, in Frederic Church's hand, OL.1981.687.

Fern Hunting among These Picturesque Mountains:
Frederic Edwin Church in Jamaica

The second exhibition in the Evelyn
and Maurice Sharp Gallery at Olana
June 6 – October 31, 2010

Curated by Evelyn D. Trebilcock and
Valerie A. Balint, with research by Ida Brier

Works in the Exhibition

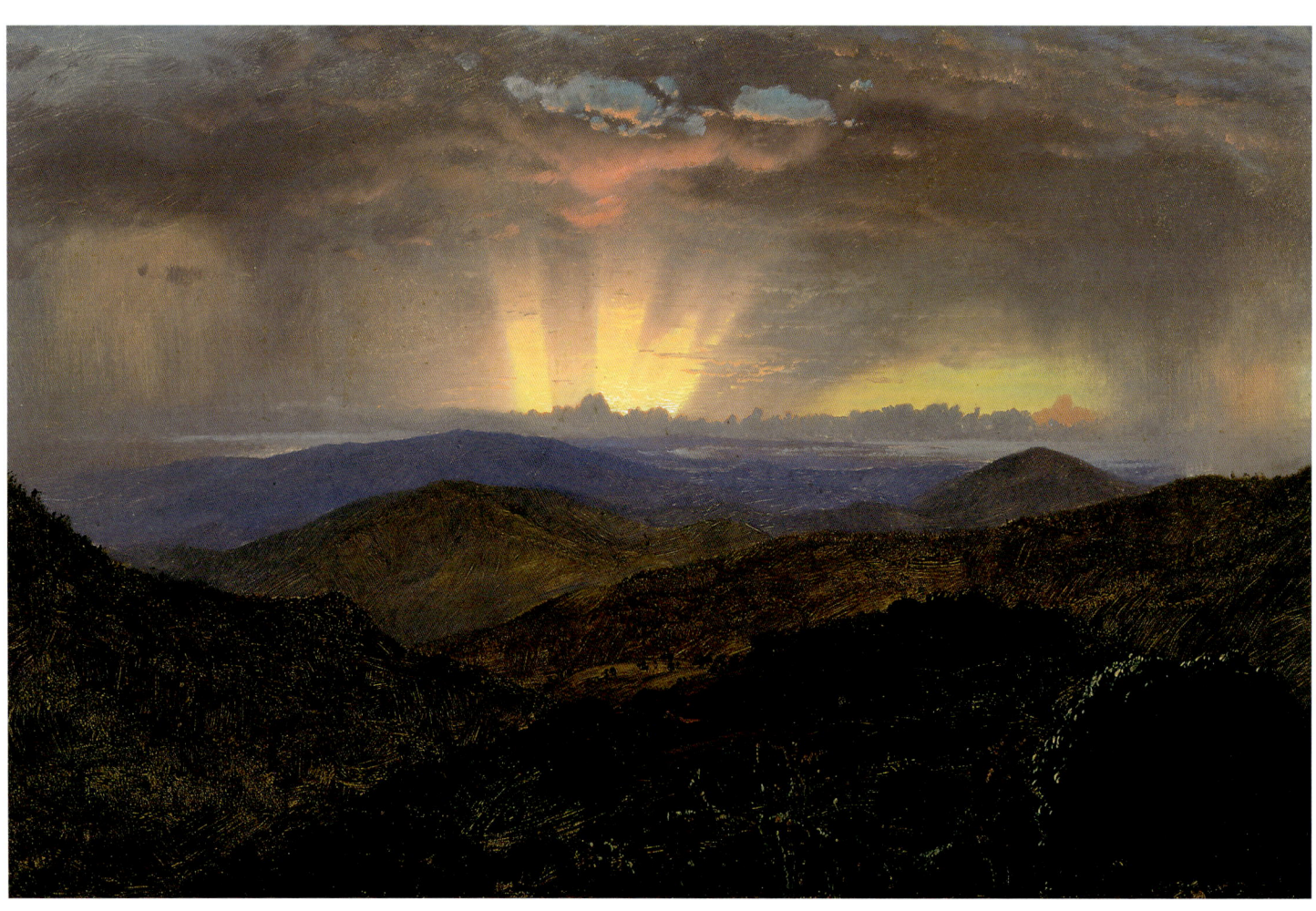

Frederic Edwin Church, *Ridges in the Blue Mountains, Jamaica*, July 1865, oil on paper, 10⅜ × 12¹⁄₁₆ in., OL.1976.3 (fig. 2)

Frederic Edwin Church, *Storm in the Blue Mountains, Jamaica*, August 1865, oil on academy board, 10 × 12¹⁄₁₆ in., OL.1976.16 (fig. 10)

Frederic Edwin Church, *Tropical Vines and Trees, Jamaica*, c. May–July 1865, oil on paper mounted on wood, 18⅛ × 12½ in., OL.1980.1948 (fig. 11)

Frederic Edwin Church, *Coconut Palms, Kingston, Jamaica*, July 7, 1865, ink on paper, 9⅞ × 7⅞ in., OL.1977.119 (fig. 12)

Frederic Edwin Church, *Fern Walk, Jamaica*, July 1865, oil on paper mounted on canvas, 12¼ × 13¼ in., OL.1981.73 (fig. 14)

Frederic Edwin Church, *Scene in the Blue Mountains, Jamaica*, August 1865, oil on paper mounted on academy board, 10⅝ × 17¾ in., OL.1981.69 (fig. 22)

Frederic Edwin Church, *Blue Mountains, Jamaica*, c. July–August 1865, oil and graphite on paper, 8¹⁄₁₆ × 12 in., OL.1976.2 (fig. 23)

Frederic Edwin Church, *Clouds in the Blue Mountains, Jamaica*, July 1865, oil on paper mounted on academy board, 11⅛ × 10¼ in., OL.1976.15 (fig. 24)

Frederic Edwin Church, *The After Glow*, November 1867, oil on canvas, 31¼ × 48¾ in., OL.1981.48 (fig. 27)

Frederic Edwin Church, *Sunset, Jamaica*, July 1865, oil on paper mounted on canvas, 12⅛ × 18⅛ in., OL.1981.26 (fig. 28)

Attributed to Marianne North, *Study of Pelican Flower, Aristolochia grandiflora*, c. March–April 1872, oil on canvas, 16⅜ × 19½ in., OL.1977.260 (fig. 36)

Martin Johnson Heade, *Tropical Orchid*, c. 1871–74, oil on canvas, 21¼ × 17¼ in., OL.1981.39 (fig. 37)

Charles de Wolf Brownell, *Royal Palm*, 1862, oil on paper mounted on canvas, 14⅜ × 10⅜ in., OL.1981.30 (fig. 38)

Unknown photographer, *Tropical Foliage, Jamaica*, c. 1870s, albumen print, 11¼ × 7⅞ in., OL.1982.1264 (fig. 45)

Unknown photographer, *Waterfall, Jamaica*, c. 1865–70, albumen print, 11¼ × 7⅞ in., OL.1982.1265 (fig. 46)

Fritz Siegfried Georg Melbye, *Entrance to the City of St. Domingo, Columbus "Tower,"* 1864, oil on canvas, 8½ × 14¼ in., OL.1980.1907 (fig. 47)

Shirley Hibberd, *The Fern Garden*, London: Groombridge and Sons, 1869, OL.1984.107 (fig. 51)

Unknown photographer, *Shore with Isthmus, Jamaica*, c. 1860s, albumen print, 7⅛ × 9 in., OL.1981.693 (fig. 52)

Unknown photographer, *Clearing in a Jungle, Jamaica*, c. 1855–65, salt print, 12⅝ × 16⅞ in., OL.1982.1256 (fig. 58)

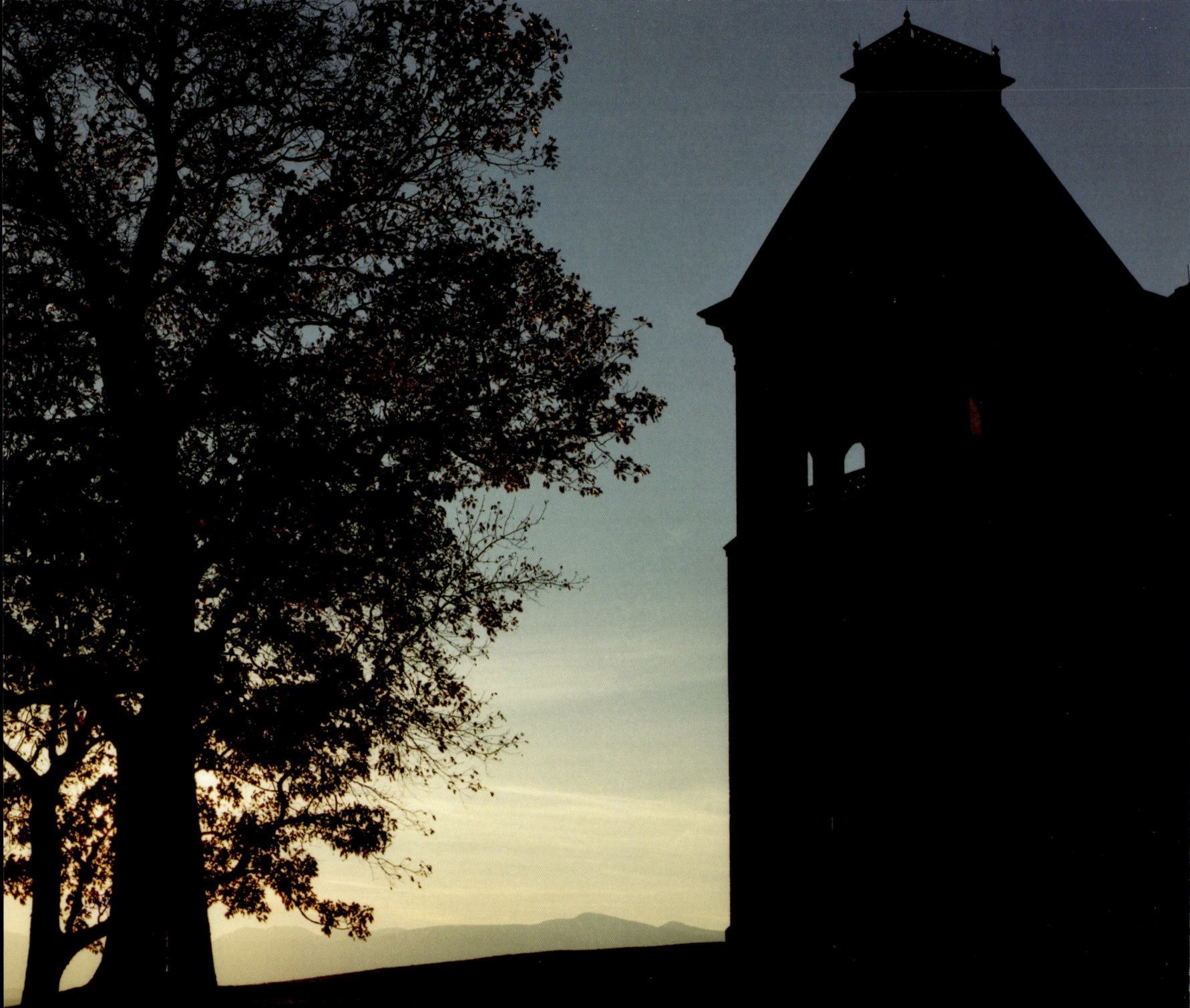

This book and the accompanying exhibition were made possible in part by generous gifts from the following:

David B. and Mimi G. Forer
Mr. and Mrs. Brock Ganeles
David G. Kabiller
Stephen and Bindy Kaye
The Lois H. and Charles A. Miller Jr. Foundation
Chas A. Miller III
The New York State Council on the Arts
   Museum Program
The Olana Exhibition Fund
The Reed Foundation
Richard T. Sharp
The Terra Foundation for American Art
The Jack Warner Fund for Creativity and Innovation
Susan Winokur and Paul Leach

We are particularly grateful to Henry and Sharon Martin for their commitment and dedication to supporting the development of high-quality catalogues in conjunction with Olana exhibitions.

The Trustees and staff of The Olana Partnership wish to recognize the support of Governor David A. Paterson; New York State Office of Parks, Recreation and Historic Preservation Commissioner Carol Ash; Deputy Commissioner for Historic Preservation J. Winthrop Aldrich; Director of the Division for Historic Preservation Ruth Pierpont; Acting Director of the Bureau of Historic Sites John Lovell; Regional Director, Taconic Region, Jayne McLaughlin; and Olana Site Manager Linda E. McLean.

The Jack Warner Fund for Creativity and Innovation was established in December 2009 to honor the work of Jonathan Westervelt Warner to advance American art through education and exhibitions. Donations to The Jack Warner Fund are used to enhance Olana's exhibitions and support Olana's education endowment. We are grateful to the many donors who made gifts to establish this fund in Jack's honor and invite you to consider making a gift.

The Evelyn and Maurice Sharp Gallery was made possible by a generous donation from Richard T. Sharp and is named in memory of his parents. Additional support was provided by Susan Winokur and Paul Leach and by The Peter Jay Sharp Foundation.

Supporting Olana

The Olana Partnership was founded in 1971 to assist and support New York State in the restoration and preservation of Olana. We rely on a large number of supporters—individuals, foundations, companies, and public sector sources—to fund our work for the enhancement of Olana and its integral viewshed, to sponsor educational programs, and to foster scholarly research on the artist and his property. This support is essential to sustain Olana's education, outreach, and public programs, to care for the collection, and to support lending from and exhibitions of the collection. Your donation will make a real difference and enable others to enjoy Olana both now and into the future. For more information on how you can help, please contact The Development Office, The Olana Partnership, PO Box 199, Hudson, NY 12534 or visit us at *www.olana.org*.

Our Mission

The Olana Partnership serves to inspire the public by preserving and interpreting Olana, Frederic Edwin Church's artistic masterpiece.

Our Vision

The fully restored Olana, vibrant with the activity of students, visitors, and scholars, will be the most widely recognized artist's home and studio in the world.

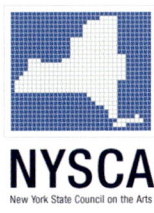

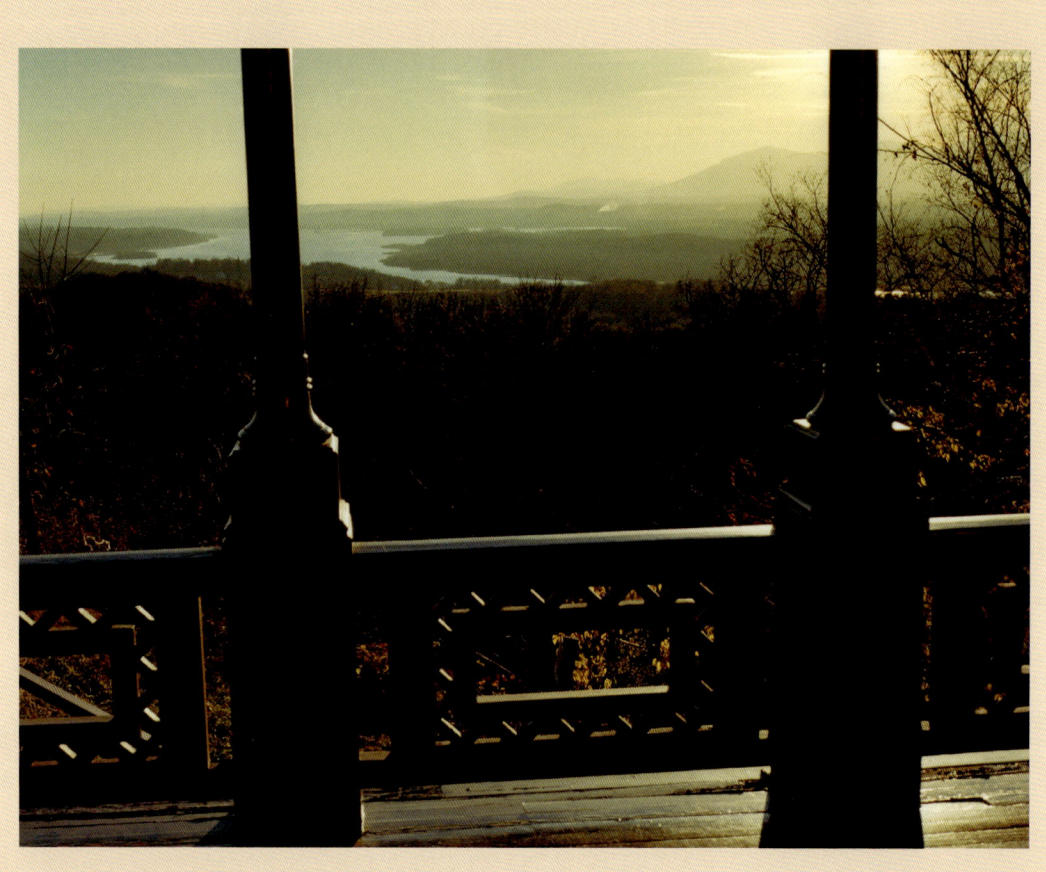

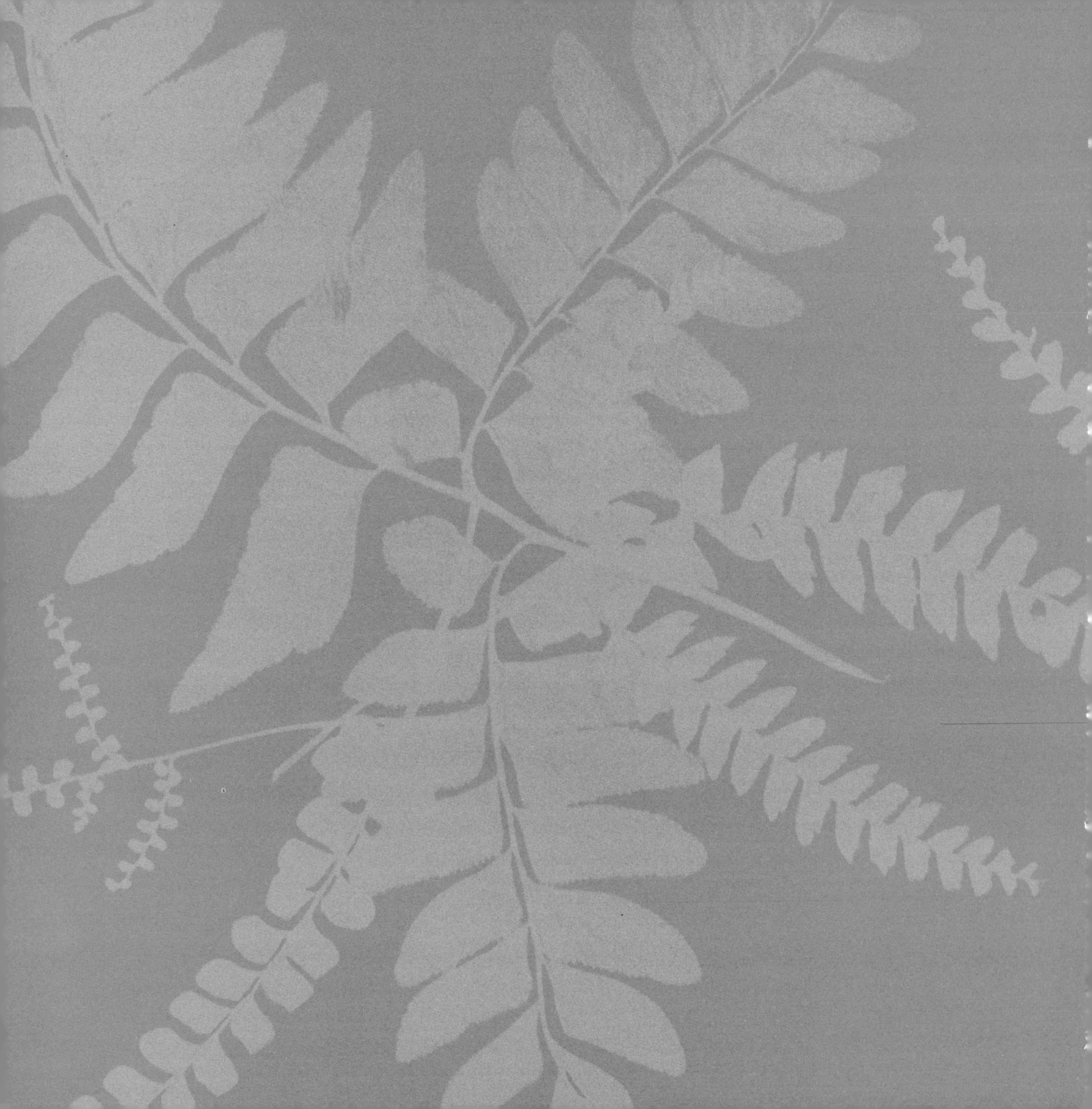